```
HQ        Stigen
773.6
S74       Heartaches and handicaps
```

SAN JOSE CITY COLLEGE LIBRARY
2100 MOORPARK AVENUE
SAN JOSE, CALIF. 95128

MAR 2 2 1977

Heartaches and Handicaps

An Irreverent Survival Manual for Parents

by Gail Stigen

Science and Behavior Books, Inc.
Palo Alto, California 94306

© Copyright 1976 by Science and Behavior Books, Inc. Printed in the United States of America. All rights reserved. This book or parts thereof may not be reproduced in any form without written permission of the Publisher.

Library of Congress Card Number 74-74561
ISBN 8314-0040-4

Typography by Penguin ≈ Santa Clara, California 95050

Dedication

This book is fondly dedicated to all parents who have had to deal with district psychologists, educators, social workers, agency directors, special education teachers, pediatricians, professionals, uninformed neighbors, relatives, in-laws, funding sources, big words, learned theories, meetings, committees, sorrow, rage, frustration, humiliation, each other, and yourselves.

Special Thanks:

to all of you cheerful, kind, and loving persons who suffered my various threshings while I was gestating this doorstop;

to my spouse, who withstood the trauma of seeing me stomp in midair and scribble something on the nearest surface when the Muse hit;

to you parents who have generously lent your experiences to me;

an especial warm gratitude to the busy administrator who gave his stern encouragement to keep me reasonably on track;

and, oh, yes, to the targets of my hurled shaft who swallowed their pride and encouraged me impartially.

(I didn't realize until now what a great group of people I know.)

Table of Contents

Foreword ix
Happy Mother's Day xi
Chapter One — Torments of the Damned 1
Chapter Two — Handicaps: An Equal
    Opportunity Employer 11
Chapter Three — Getting Help or Services........... 25
Chapter Four — Social Workers..................... 33
Chapter Five — Special Education................. 45
Chapter Six — My Sibling, The Savage.............. 59
Chapter Seven — Establishing Carpools and
    Other Traps.. 67
Chapter Eight — Special Stories and Special Olympics . 79
Chapter Nine — Religion and some *Do*'s and *Don't*s ... 93
Chapter Ten — Meetings 103
Chapter Eleven — Understanding State Agencies..... 111
Final Facts 117
Conclusion 123

Foreword

Gail Stigen's book reminds me of something that I tend to forget. Her humorous, abrasive, first-hand account focuses attention on an important issue. Most of us are very uncomfortable with differentness, with injuries, with handicaps, particularly in the young. We avoid unpleasantness sometimes by refusing to see, sometimes by euphemisms, and often by institutionalized care. We are more comfortable if we can account for tragedy as somehow the fault of the other. Somehow these people are different and deserve their fate. The idea of a random universe is frightening to most of us.

The parents of the mentally handicapped seem as ready to accept their role as we are to give it to them. Gail Stigen seems to accept nothing. She refuses to be stigmatized. Her salvation is humor — fast-moving slapstick that throws off old methods of categorization and standard procedure. She refuses to be pitied or intimidated. Well-meaning and usually well-paid professionals including psychiatrists like myself had better take warning. We must do more to increase our efforts to make sense and produce results.

For her iconoclastic leadership Gail Stigen might well be compared to Ralph Nader and Betty Friedan. It is hard to think of anyone to whom to compare her humor. Behind the laughter and exaggeration and outrage there is self-doubt and pain and confusion. She shares them all without apology.

Robert S. Spitzer, M.D.
Editor-in-Chief

HAPPY MOTHER'S DAY

When I had my first child, I knew I had a baby as all first mothers know what a baby is. What first mothers often don't know is what first babies are supposed to do or not do.

Believe me when I say my daughter had the best of everything from conception on. I was a regular Mother Nature type. The obstetrician had his hands full with me.

Both my doctor and my husband put up with my bright ideas such as the "suitcase" I packed for my husband for his trip to the hospital. I thought he should have some comforts, too, and the admitting office found itself faced with a determined woman in advanced stages of labor, hissing, "No, I'm keeping *this* bag," and hanging on to it. We went through all the preliminaries of labor and my husband was allowed in the labor room where I proudly handed him the suitcase.

He very gravely inspected the contents and thanked me for including the latest bestseller, a flacon of sherry (the best), a knife for the cheese and salami; he admired my taste in crackers, and said he could use the aspirin.

So I had the baby. Money was no object. Care of both Mom and babe was excellent.

A slight problem with baby's foot? Quick! The best orthopedic man around. Solved.

Wardrobe? Guess, reader. Right.

All visits to the pediatrician were on schedule including one on New Year's Day for a three-sneeze siege.

We were hairtrigger parents when it came to the candy kid.

As a chronic over-achiever, I started reading Progress Charts. Both my husband and pediatrician assured me there was a wide latitude on the plus or minus side and development shouldn't be rigidly plotted.

This reassurance soothed me for three years. Then the mother/bitch in me said, *"Something is not on schedule."* So permission was granted to run some preliminary tests — just as a matter of course.

I felt like Judas leading a lamb astray (don't bother about mixed metaphors) the day I took my child for the first visit. Since this procedure can be long and drawn out, we sort of floated through the months of appointments. As a matter of fact, I did have another minor distraction: a handsome son. This particular young mother had a helluva time what with one child having an EEG while the other was being breastfed. I became a super scheduler as setting up baby-sitters was a full-time job. Thank the powers that be that I had a very flexible group.

So the tests continued. One Wednesday in May our daughter had the sniffles, so was taken to the pediatrician. As I walked in the door he asked me how I was. I replied that I was just fine, thank you, but the baby had a fever. At that point the doctor interrupted me and said, "You don't know your child is brain damaged — or actually ideopathic, retardation, severe?"

All I heard was "brain damage," something "retardation" and "severe." The rest was a daze, but we made an appointment for the following Sunday so the doctor could talk to both my husband and me at the same time.

I don't recall driving home, but I do recall trying to get a baby-sitter for Sunday. As it was Mother's Day, and all my sitters were honoring their own mothers, I had to stay home. I decided not to tell my husband because I hadn't even got the whole story, and felt a garbled version would only make matters worse.

Sunday arrived and my husband drove off to the doctor alone. It was one of the more sickening events of my life, watching that man drive off to hear that the fluffy rose of his life was retarded.

When he returned, he just looked at me a long, silent time and said, "Happy Mother's Day."

Needless to say, we endure, rather than observe Mother's Day around here.

Chapter One

Torments of the Damned

I recall the days following my child's diagnosis, when I would watch the other neighborhood children from the front window — a pillar of agony, alone and isolated. I felt outraged that as a result of fate I would have to reveal my soul to persons known as professionals because my child needed special care. In ordinary circumstances I would have decked anyone asking me some of the questions I got asked, but now I had to submerge my ego to help my issue.

What pulled me out of this dangerous whirlpool was boredom. That's right, boredom. This tearstained, headachy person with the blank stare *bored* me. I found that I was boring myself and thought "Good God, what I must be doing to my family!" All of them. I looked around. I was a mess, the house was a mess, my children were retreating into unknown worlds, and then I discovered another puddle of misery; in my selfish entrapment I had neglected to notice that there was another human being who had as much invested in this child as I. My spouse. Every day he went into the public arena acting as if nothing had happened.

When a human being is diagnosed "handicapped" there is no obituary, so the public doesn't know you're in mourning. When a dear one dies, you see him dead; nice things are said and it becomes a *final* fact. There is no getting around it. It's there, like it or not.

When a brain, a limb, or a system is dead, but the body is alive, then you experience living death — a very long-term assignment. As a matter of fact, it lasts your entire lifetime in most cases.

I pulled out of my spin in three weeks. I'm lucky. However, it has given me several character traits; I smoke too much, I probably drink too much, I am as testy as an asp when confronted with whines of no importance. I also get an expression of impending nausea when faced with lies and unfulfilled promises. I have become a fierce fighter against professional and bureaucratic inequities and ineptitude, not only for myself, but for the parents of other handicapped children as well. In short, I got off my ass and started to work.

I started this journey timidly enough. A neighbor who saw my anguish but didn't know what to do (actually she did, but didn't know where to start) was relieved when I finally asked her if she knew anyone with a similar problem. As this warm, loving woman knew practically everyone, she was able to direct me to a mother with similar problems. This mother and I were peers, yet she had had years of experience. She found me one day standing on her doorstep like an orphan. She heard my stumbling questions and saw my beaten stance. She immediately dropped everything she had planned for that day and gave me a cram course. I don't even remember what she looked like, and in my state at the time I doubt if I even thanked her, but I shall never forget her help.

After that there was a series of incidents which I found enraging, bewildering, challenging, and time consuming. But it was productive. I may be ignorant, but I am not stupid and was able to understand (if not predict) what was ahead. The struggle was on. The family settled into a routine, accepting sitters, etc., while I searched. As a matter of fact, my husband made me the envy of the Corporation! I had a janitorial service once a month for the heavy cleaning, a bimonthly cleaning woman, a babysitter four times a week during the day, and more if I needed it. This took money. Well, he made it and I spent it. It was for our child. He knew his hard-earned money wasn't going for clothes because I looked like a slob. But I was one of the lucky ones. I could afford the above help. I suspect that most mothers aren't so fortunate.

During this period, reader, I was burying my dead, being a corporation wife, functioning as a member of the human race, reading books, entertaining, etc. Also, do not forget, my husband was holding up his part of the bargain. Some bargain.

Anyhow, we did it. Our "normal" child proved to give us the biggest run for our money, so to speak. Our son had six major operations in two years, starting at the age of four. And guess who was terrified at the prospect of another invalid in the family? Well, I resisted the urge to spoil him and now he's the healthiest kid on the block.

Speaking of remaining children without handicaps, I'm known as the neighborhood madwoman because I cannot *stand* to see these healthy, whole children trying to get maimed or killed through carelessness. *Random* causes can cripple one for life frequently enough without going out and courting disaster.

I find the look of pity that crosses people's faces when they learn we have a handicapped child quite disconcerting. It's sort of like being the permanent survivor at a funeral of life. I'm not really seeking sympathy when I acknowledge my own child.

Do you keep your child and affliction a secret? It's tempting. Why? Well, again, some examples might help. The most unnerving one to me occurred when I was working as a volunteer on a physical therapy project with a severely involved cerebral palsy victim who had above average intelligence. We were chatting about this and that as we went through our routines and this person asked me how I got into this particular field. I replied that I had a handicapped child and mentioned the diagnosis. This person immediately looked shattered with sorrow, touched my arm and with great feeling apologized for intruding on my privacy. My mind blew! Here was a person who couldn't move without outside aid feeling sorry for *me*. The experience of this person's empathy was overwhelming.

Another time I was larking about at a party and one woman who was admiring my monologue said it must be nice to be so free of cares in life that I could project such freedom of spirit. I glanced at my husband and saw him turn grey. Someone quickly took this woman aside and hastily whispered that we had this problem child. I was then in the position of being the Pagliacci of the cocktail set — a role I care nothing for.

I don't mind discussing my child. Really. I can be quite frank about her, too. I know she is quite beautiful. I also know that my child doesn't have many brain cells working. That's not a bid for pity; that's a fact.

We parents develop a sort of gallows humor. The women seem to be better versed in the black humor that evolves and I think it is because we are more on the firing line level. Also, women have had the primitive experience of childbirth and have a better chance.

I make only brief mention of my husband. There is a reason for this. I envision his mind as a private heap of grief. I tend to use the whole world for group therapy so I can reduce the tensions built up in me. That isn't his bag. He is a tungsten-coated marshmallow who must seek his own coping patterns. He hasn't read, and probably won't read this book.

It may appear that mothers are always the first to hear. Not true. Many obstetricians tend to blurt out the bad news to the father while the mother is still recovering from childbirth. I happened to see such a drama personally. The father was standing in the hall of the hospital, waiting to see his wife. The doctor came out, still suited up from the delivery, took the guy aside, told him that his baby was extremely handicapped, and that his signature was needed immediately. I watched this man go through the ritualistic bureaucracies of life — and then the nurse told him that he could see his wife. My mind rejected the ensuing scene.

Discovering the concrete fact that you have a handicapped child is a heart-stopping, mindboggling, gut-level body blow. Some parents get it socked to them right at birth. Others get it later. Some accept it, some reject it, some buckle under the strain, some rise above the fact.

All are consumed with an awful sorrow. Not the surgical sorrow of death, but an hourly, daily, yearly sorrow — an agonizing, shattering, tearing sorrow.

Frequently, while writing this book (I did it all in longhand), I had the urge to just scribble in red ink (the color of blood), put the cap on my pen, and my sobbing head on the table. Then this voice would whisper to me, "Sit Up! Remember your own big advice — remember the sobbing wretches you've held in your arms while they were being torn apart. Remember your resolution that crying isn't going to help your child. Remember that you aren't the only one who has seen her beloved child handicapped. Remember, remember, remember, but don't live memories, live *life*. You must! Martyrdom went out with the catapult and rock. And never forget that you have other equally important responsibilities and you are not going to wreck all of that because of a random accident of fate."

In our "handicapped world" there are many persons who have selflessly devoted years of time and energy on our behalf, and are legendary in their effectiveness. I personally have gained immensely by following their direction and advice. Recently, I found my name on a list for achievement nominations, along with several of these persons, which led to a mutual teasing. They insisted that I was certainly coming up in the world and that if I continued to follow their advice I too might become a "living legend." All in good fun, of course. As I move through each crisis, I share my triumphs and tribulations with them and we have evolved the habit of greeting each other with "Hi, how's the 'LL' today?" or, "Is this the county achiever?" and other irreverencies. This in no way diminishes our respect for each other, it just simplifies communication.

One of these "Living Legends" gave me a path to follow — and not an easy one, either. This was years ago and has proven 100 per cent correct. I was discussing this book with her recently and she asked me if I had described sorrow. Well, I've mentioned sorrow, but I haven't yet described it. Sorrow is your child's birthday. Sorrow is seeing your child beaten, stoned, and spit upon. Sorrow is going into your child's empty room at night, drawing the shades, saying goodnight to the vacant bed, turning off the lights that shine on nothing and softly closing the door so as not to disturb the spirit that sleeps in that room. A room full of your child. A room as barren as your empty arms, as barren as your aching breasts that nourished this child — as barren as the look on your husband's face.

That is sorrow, reader, and all of us live with this 60 seconds a minute, 60 minutes an hour, 24 hours a day, 7 days a week, 4.3 weeks a month, 12 months a year, every year, and we will live with it the rest of our lives.

Imagine any variation of the Gethsemane that all parents go through when told that their child has a problem and you will have a glimpse of a contemporary

Dante's inferno; an embarkation on the river Styx* with only hope left in Pandora's Box.

The parents endure. How they endure is due solely to their own inner resources. They all come to realize that the world has stopped. The future looms bleak.

"I'm so alone in my anguish" is the silent cry.

Not so. Out there — not too far away — are those comforting arms; the gentle, compassionate voice; the glimmer of others seen through the tears; the first tiny, timid, apologetic joke; the first rage which is accepted as earned; the smiling person who comes to you and says, "Follow our path, you are not alone."

Then the parent is ready to get up out of the pit of despair and look around. It is the Alpha but not the Omega of their work. They have work ahead. Hard work.

This living legend woman I mentioned earlier told me she had the unenviable task of having interviewed over 10,000 sets of parents for out-of-home placement and said she wished she could make up some huge cloak to put around the parents to protect them from further sorrow and pain. She told me there was not one single parent who was not suffering the torments of the damned. She said she knows that these parents are going to face life having this pain further exacerbated by the professionals whom they will encounter and she feels helpless that she can't provide a shield or a mantle of protection.

But what makes me so impatient is the professional "help" for me. *I* don't need it. My child does. Let's get to

---

*It is actually the Rubicon, but we don't know this yet, reader.

work. Forget what caused this. Let's make it run as well as possible. I'm for letting the geneticists and theologians research prevention. I'm involved in the present and the future.

What follows will be a book describing some of the things that can happen to a parent when one steps through the mirror of having a handicapped child. The goal I want firmly fixed in the mind of the reader is that this is a book about being a *parent*. It will be part textbook, part history, part reminiscence, part teaching, part learning, and entirely true.

The book may not appear logical as the author is as odd as a brass piano (and built somewhat similarly). As the reader moves through the book he or she will notice that the author uses the shaft rather than the needle.

So come with me on a journey through this world. It is a world that at first seems numbingly lonely and isolated, but emerges as a very hard-working, humorous, and warm world — a world populated with human beings.

Chapter Two

Handicaps: An Equal Opportunity Employer

I was most reluctant to do this chapter, but it has been repeatedly suggested that I give some diagnostic definitions. At first I felt unqualified. I still don't feel *qualified*, but a small incident happened to me that made me think that a brief amateur interpretation might be helpful. I was talking with the mother of a child who had a well-known, easily diagnosed handicap. She was doing volunteer work and had just been exposed to a group of children who didn't appear to have anything wrong with them. She was quite amazed to see them in a "handicapped" program and her subsequent lack of knowledge made me wonder if we *all* don't have gaps in our understanding of various handicaps.

Be warned. To date I have not been declared the Oracle of Handicaps and this is only my interpretation of the various definitions. May I add that in researching this chapter I found out that various authorities often don't agree with each other, with the parents, the teachers, relatives, or anyone else?

My hope is that this chapter will point up the reason that there is so much bewildered, taut uncertainty around in our handicapped world. Also, I will freely admit that it is an emotionally exhausting kind of research. But don't bleed internally for me. If you want to spare a moment of contemplation, contemplate the parents caught in the grey area of diagnoses. Emotionally, it is like living on the epicenter of an active earthquake fault.

One mother really got it between the eyes. Her little boy was in and out of diagnostic evaluations for years — everywhere. The evaluations varied enough to keep the parents looking further. He was enrolled in a pre-school for suspected-but-not-confirmed problems. After he had been there for about six weeks, the director made an appointment with the mother. His opening line was, "Your son is severely disturbed and the prognosis is dim."

The mother only recalls being held in someone's arms outside the center and being hustled off somewhere by a soothing-voiced pair. After being driven to someone's house, given a pill and a stiff shot of whiskey, she realized that a couple of parents (at the school to pick up their own child) had fielded her as she stood looking wildly around the parking lot — rooted in shock. These were veteran parents and knew precisely what they were seeing. They had known this woman's hopes for a minor problem in her son and when they saw her expression, they knew immediately that those hopes were shattered. They also realized she could get killed trying to drive home in such a state.

Once having rescued her, they were able to advise her on techniques of breaking the news at home and other hard-learned lessons. She was driven home, given a hot bath, and put to bed. She handled the situation like a champ. And years later she is able to laugh that she — a nurse yet — was so rattled that she let someone take her home and give her liquor and pills without a protest.

So, the parents know they have a problem. The next step is to discover the extent of the problem. And a lot of problems develop trying to discover the extent of the problem.

When I realized that we had a problem I promptly went to the library and read *every* book on the subject I could find. After researching this chapter years later, and re-reading these books, it is with wonder I didn't take the hands of my family and lead them in a lemming-like odyssey to the sea.

My God. The maze of terms, the coldly stated theories that bear no human application, the arch attitudes, the condescending tones, and the conflicting schools of thought. The real lack of empathy has gotten me alternating between blind rage and an awe of the "real" people we deal with daily on a positive basis.

Autism. To me this is one of the most wrenching disabilities or diagnoses going. I also think it is the least understood, and the least served. The next time you are feeling sorry for yourself, reader, call the mother of an autistic child (the Society is usually listed in the phone book) and ask her how things are going. Explain that you are feeling blue because your child didn't pass second grade calculus. Perhaps this is a negative reflection on you as a parent?

Well, if the conversation doesn't bring you to your knees with compassion, then you weren't listening.

Bluntly, autism is childhood schizophrenia. Generally (please note that I say "generally" quite frequently, as it is a case of "four out of five doctors say...") there are fourteen signs indicative of a true autistic child. If there are seven of the signs present a diagnosis of autism is made. They are:

1. Not a cuddly baby. (A very real characteristic that is looked for first; it raises hell with the mother's psyche.)
2. Acts as deaf.
3. Overactivity (hyperactivity).
4. Fetishism (an obsessive attachment to an object).
5. No eye contact.
6. Spinning of objects.
7. Repetitive play.
8. Standoffish manners.
9. Great difficulty playing and relating with other children.
10. Resists change of routine.
11. Gestures only — no verbal communication.
12. Harsh, wild, shrill laughter for no reason.
13. Lacks fear of real dangers (some doctors say they feel there is more danger awareness than is usually assumed).
14. Resistance to learning.

The outlook and prognosis is generally poor and according to some if there is no communication by five years of age it is indeed a bad picture. Language is just one facet of communication, bear in mind. The cause is unknown. It could be biochemical, organic, neurological disorder, a variation of retardation, or just a developed behavior.

Now armed with this list and an urge to play amateur diagnostician, go to your local playground and check out the children. No, they are not *all* autistic; it just seems that way. A conservative estimate of diagnosed autistic children in this country is 25,000. Notice I say "diagnosed autistic children." The mind reels to consider the countless thousands in the boondocks who have not been diagnosed — where the word "autism" is unknown.

Mental Retardation is, I think, the biggest single category of handicaps in the world. I *know* it has the poorest image and the worst press. In addition, Mental Retardation is constantly being lumped together with Mental Illness. They are as different as day and night.

One can be retarded and not cerebral palsied, or one can be cerebral palsied and retarded; or one can have epilepsy without retardation; or one can be cerebral palsied with epilepsy and retardation; or one can have a genetic imbalance that makes one automatically retarded; or one can get a disease that will cause retardation; or one can sustain an injury leaving brain damage and retardation; or one can be emotionally disturbed, causing retardation; or, or, or.

A reasonably accepted definition of mental retardation is given by the American Association on Mental

Deficiency: "Mental retardation refers to significantly subaverage general intellectual functioning existing concurrently with deficits in adaptive behavior, and manifested during the developmental period."

In other words, you're not making it on schedule.

Due to more sophisticated testing and heightened awareness of problem areas today, more children are being examined more closely. However, this is not without its problems. A label of retardation can be a convenient label when there seems no explainable reason for lack of development. Minority groups are *vividly* aware of the inherent dangers of such testing. My own experience might be a case in point.

Through an oversight I was allowed to watch my child getting one of those tests. The kid was extremely young and being a first child had been given a lot of love and bathing but not much exposure to "life." I didn't know what I was watching at the time. But, believe me, I do now. "Show me the choo choo." At home we called them trains and in our area they were as rare as the Great Auk egg. In a playhouse setting it was "show me the baby." No reaction. None from me either. I didn't see a baby, I saw a doll.

There must have been some point to all this — oh, yes — testing isn't infallible and thank the powers that be, IQ tests are being scrutinized more carefully. As a matter of fact, in the last three years or so, several pieces of legislation have been enacted to protect the indiscriminate use of such tests.

As I see it, Mental Retardation revolves on an axis of IQ. (I'll probably catch hell from somebody for that statement.) There are degrees of retardation and these are based on IQ levels ranging from "Profound" to "Mild."*

But onward with definitions. Mental Retardation. My dictionary defines retardation thusly: 1. Retard. 1: to make slow or slower; impede. 2: to delay academic progress by failure to promote, to undergo retardation. syn: see Delay. 2. Retard n: a holding back or slowing down: Retardation — serving or tending to retard — retardant n.

Retardate: One who is mentally retarded (a really awful word).

Retardation: n 1: an act or instance of retarding. 2: the extent to which anything is retarded. 3a: an abnormal slowness of thought or action; b: slowness in development or progress.

Retarded adj: slow or limited in intellectual or emotional development or academic progress."

It is interesting to note that the next word in my dictionary is "retch," a tendency some people have upon encountering mental retardation for the first time. We know that all babies are darling, those of elementary school age are tolerated, but to come face to face with retardation at the adult level can be harrowing for the uninitiated. Why? Let me examine my soul here for a minute and perhaps I can explain.

---

*While writing this, it occurred to me in a flash of intelligence that most people don't realize Retardation is an IQ measurement, rather than a disease. "Retardation" is a really powerful stigma that slams the door of opportunity in the face of any person with the label. I contend that if everybody got tested, the total number of MR persons would resemble the national debt.

I think it is the look in the eyes. You find yourself exchanging a glance with another human being and it suddenly dawns on you that you are peering into the face of perfect honesty — an experience for which most of us are totally unprepared.

You *know* with the retarded where you stand. Let there be no question about that. I know of one program in which the community coordinator was uncomfortable around anyone else with less than intellectual perfection. She would enter the room and as if by magic there suddenly would be no children; and only a glazed-looking staff. The retarded have an uncanny ability for being able to sense when rejection is in the air. It's called "vibes" these days. We all know when we are in a hostile environment, and so do they. Even more so. I would use a mentally retarded person any day as a bellweather to let me know when there was a phony in our midst. It rarely fails.

I have a mind like a bird in an aviary — always jumping from branch to branch. Where were we? Oh, definitions.

There are a number of MR diagnoses characterized by certain physical signs. The most widely known, I think, is Downs Syndrome, or Mongoloids. Whoever coined the term "Mongoloid" should be boiled in oil before being drawn and quartered. It is perfectly all right to be a Mongoloid in Mongolia, but a disaster to be one anywhere else. (I know it's Mongolian, but I think the point stands.) Downs Syndrome is defined as a genetic imbalance. My handy dandy dictionary really falls down here, describing it as a "congenital idiocy of unknown ultimate cause in which a child is born with slanting eyes, a broad, short skull and broad hands with short fingers."

That definition alone should put legions of parents into irreversible depression. I didn't think the word "idiocy" was used anymore, but to my surprise I was recently told by a student in special education that the professor seriously informed the class that levels of retardation were categorized as "morons," "idiots," and "vegetables." I knew the student well enough to know that she wasn't exaggerating. She was also smart enough to wait until she got her grade from this 13th century teacher before registering a huge complaint about him. We are all afraid of "grudge grading."

Downs children may be born to older women or to younger women, good women and bad women, active women and passive women. Downs Syndrome does not respect economic status, nor does it have any prejudices due to skin color. There is only one point on which all authorities agree, and that is the old cliché that only women can bear Downs children.

If I seem a bit edgy here, reader, it's probably my conscience. When I was a kid (centuries ago) I remember inflicting countless verbal atrocities on a child named Sally who was lonesome — and mongoloid. Oh, my, we were so perfect. Poor Sally had to put up with our morning and afternoon forays past her house because it was on the way to the park — a logical destination for the jackal pack that we were. We never missed the opportunity to taunt her when she came out to wave to us. Sally's mother was probably engraving the wall with her fingernails in agony at the rejection of the fruit of her womb trying to make contact with such barbarians.

Ask me today which group of handicapped give me the most pleasure and I would have to say the Downs kids. And not only children, because modern medicine has made it possible for these persons to have a longer life span and today one sees more and more older persons with Downs Syndrome. They have also emerged from the Stygian gloom of utter rejection to achieving many, many accomplishments.

Because of their uniform characteristics the inexperienced would logically say they all look alike. I discovered quite by accident that that is *not* true. I had known a family for some time on a personal level and was in a position to teach their Downs kid something. But he was *not* going to be taught, and that's all there was to it. I was fed up with *all* children that day and was equally determined that he *was* going to learn. Well, there we both were, eyeball to eyeball, locked on a collision course of egos, when I suddenly found myself shouting at him, "Damn it, Mark, don't you *dare* give me that rotten pig-headed look your father gets when he's mad." Mark was a dead ringer for his old man at that moment and it was obvious! This simple discovery prompted me to try and match parents with their children, and vice versa. Now I can almost recognize the parent after knowing the child and his/her various traits. As all of us experts do occasionally, I did fail to identify a child with his parents, but later realized that this was the *cute* kid of a couple for whom I cared little.

I also know a secret. I know at least two Downs kids who are snug as bugs in rugs because no one realizes that they are mongoloids.

Cretinism is caused by a thyroid deficiency and has certain physical characteristics, as does Hurler's syndrome. They both automatically come under the MR label.*

Three per cent of our total population (somewhat over SIX MILLION persons, for those of us who don't know what the total population is) are MR labeled. One hundred twenty-six thousand babies are born every year who will at some time be regarded as Mentally Retarded. For those of you fortunate enough to possess pocket calculators, start totaling some of these figures.

I once saw a rather lucid diagram depicting the overlap of Cerebral Palsy, Epilepsy, and Mental Retardation. It looked like this:

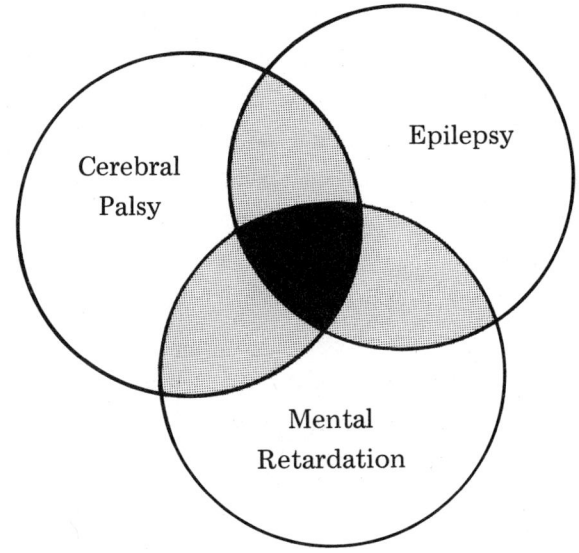

---

*As a matter of fact, I have just been told that there are almost *150* etiologies that automatically come under the MR label.

Cerebral Palsy (CP) is a brain disability resulting in muscular incoordination and speech disturbances. CP victims can have the entire range of intelligence. Also, Cerebral Palsy can range in degree from mild to severe. One doesn't die from Cerebral Palsy, and most cases will show improvement over the years. Some of the problems can be modified with surgery, and physical therapy is invaluable. Sufferers of CP are rejected publicly because of inability to control certain muscles, which makes them unacceptable in a society that does not wish to be reminded of deformities. For the life of me I cannot find a cause for CP that I can understand. I vaguely sense that it is a birth accident, but one book mentioned something about Rh incompatibility in the parents, but then got bogged down with extra-pyramidal tracts and I got left behind. There seems to be no question that CP affects the normal progress of a child and that is why there is often an overlap into the MR label.

Epilepsy is a disorder characterized by a disturbance in the body's central nervous system which takes the form of seizures that can go from the unnoticeable to the very obvious. Medication can be used effectively to control these seizures. Twenty-five per cent of MR persons have seizures. I once heard a speaker bemoaning the fact that epileptic persons were not regarded "normal" just because they had seizures. As tolerant as I thought I had become, I simply couldn't agree with him 100 per cent because I have been scared out of my wits when faced with a seizure. This is without a doubt a very real handicap, if only from the standpoint that the victim might be insensitive enough to have a seizure in public, causing someone inconvenience or embarrassment.

Muscular Dystrophy, Multiple Sclerosis, and so on are all handicaps, but if I went into each and every known handicap we would be here all night. Besides, it is not my purpose here to cover specific handicaps and their impact on everyone affected. Rather, my purpose is to show what some of the familial problems are that evolve from handicaps. If I don't achieve this purpose, I am quite sure it will be pointed out to me. Chapter and verse.

At the beginning of this chapter I made several flat statements (don't bother to mention that this whole book is a "flat statement") and I'm willing to eat a little crow. As a matter of fact, during my checkered career as "Mrs. Instant Opinion" I have had to eat a lot of crow so have developed my own personal recipe called "Crow au vin" — an acquired taste.

I have knocked some books. I also said that autism was my idea of the worst handicap. Well, I'm going to make a right angle turn. I'll put Autism on par with Brain Damage and go on to mention that Wm. Cruickshank's book on the subject, entitled *The Brain-Injured Child in Home, School, and Community* as a human explanation with understandable definitions.

Brain Injuries have been given several terms — as usual, and all of them frightening — and according to Dr. Cruickshank, they all boil down to the same thing. Some of them he lists include minimal brain-injured, brain-damaged, hyperkinetic, hyperactive, learning disabilities, dyslexia, muturational lag, perceptually disabled, and many, many other terms.

I sometimes think that if each of us were given a

diagnostic work-up, we would discover that we all belong in one big brotherhood — the brotherhood of handicaps.

There is dawning on the horizon of logic a term that seems to embrace much of the above into one single literate, understandable talking point. It is called Developmental Disabilities. Isn't that simplicity itself!

This is a matrix definition due to the fact that it evolves from Public Law 91-517, which is at the Federal level and each state tailors it to fit the individual state's needs. Also true to form, it is dabbled with and tinkered at each year thus changing the original form. Still, the following takes in all the basics:

> The developmental disabilities of mental retardation, cerebral palsy, and epilepsy are not disease entities, but are conditions characterized by an aggregation of symptoms resulting from many different causes — biological, psychological, educational, cultural, economic — which result in impaired intellectual or adaptive behavior.
>
> The disability can originate in childhood and may continue over a lifetime. Two or more of these disabilities may co-exist in one person, or a developmentally disabled person may have blindness or deafness and thereby be multiply handicapped. Persons having these disabilities often have need for residential services, education, health, vocational training, employment, recreation, and guardianship or protective services.

You can almost understand the definition, too. Isn't that amazing! Hurrah for Developmental Disabilities — a starting point.

Chapter Three
Getting Help or Services

A letter to the *San Francisco Chronicle*, January 7, 1973:

"As parents of a seven-year-old rubella youngster who is multi-handicapped, we have found that lack of services and facilities for the handicapped was not nearly the problem as the inability to find the services.

We recall only too grimly the hopelessness we encountered six and seven years ago when we began attempting to find out 'where to go,' 'what to do,' and 'whom to see.' "

(signed)
Mrs. S.L.M.
Palo Alto, Ca.

You are not alone, mother.

Have you ever said, "Boy, I could write a book about that?"

Some time after reading the above letter I found myself saying *just* that. I had been waiting in a "Professional Library" for an interview and knew it was going to be some time before I was going to be liberated. But before going on, let me give you a little background.

I am an unashamed reading addict. I'll read practically anything; want ads, fillers in the Yellow Pages, ingredients in breakfast cereals — you name it, I'll read it. Thus, as my reading habit started to get to me, I stumbled blank eyed to the shelves to get my fix — a book. They had everything there. I quickly passed by "The Problems of Dynamic Creep," "The Interface Reliability of Oil Impregnation as Pertains to Silicon Shield of Xenon Flash Lamp Pumping Ruby Lasers." I was about to give up in despair at "Altimeters and Their Place in Reproduction with Guidance and Control," when I came upon "Parents of Handicapped Children — Their Feelings and Reactions."

Ah ha! *There* was something I knew about — on the firing line level. So I read it.

I don't know which parents this esoteric manual had found to interview, but they didn't appear to be even remotely similar to anyone *I* knew. What a bunch of whimpering, guilt-ridden, uninformed, misinformed, snowed, intimidated, documented mice. These apologetic, forelock tugging supplicants at the altar of professionalism were certainly NOT the parents I have come to know, love, and admire.

Upon finishing this hardbound, expensive tome I decided that surely there should be a rebuttal, or at least another angle of approach. And that is what you are now holding in your hands.

But getting back to Help or Services. We are now at the point where we know there is a problem, and what the problem is. So the next step is to get this so-called help and services for the child, right?

Wrong.

The next step is to assume the appropriate role. This is called "masking" by writers of ponderous volumes on behavior. Getting mentally prepared to seek services requires the patience of Job, the push of Patton, the gall of Henry VIII, the sunny disposition of a badger, the self-control of a Tasmanian Devil, a head shaped like a telephone, and ten thousand shares in Ma Bell.

Then, and only then, is the parent ready.

Generally, mothers get stuck with this task as it is part of their job description. Fathers are kept busy earning enough money to pay for any services that are found. And the only thing cheap about special services is talk. Being poor helps somewhat; being rich eliminates financial worry; being in the middle is expensive. Being *anywhere* still means there is going to be a hassle finding services. Quality is merely serendipity here.

One parent asked her pediatrician what the next step was, now that she knew her child had a problem. He answered that nothing was really necessary until the child showed signs of changes. That made perfectly good sense — until she thought about it. Back to the pediatrician. "The kid's bored and should be getting some stimulation, or *something!*" Actually, doctors can be very nice about things like this. He readily admitted that he wasn't too up on special services, but would be interested in anything the parent came up with that would make him more knowledgeable.

Back to the old drawing board.

The mother then came across an article in the local blatt mentioning a fund-raising affair for children with handicaps similar to those of her child. She called the chairman and poured out her story. The chairman was most understanding and promised to mail her literature immediately, which she did. The "literature" turned out to be application forms for volunteer work at the agency, as well as information describing the benefits of working with these less advantaged persons, etc.

Hardly what she had asked for, but it *was* a start.

After innumerable phone calls mother finally managed to circumvent the volunteer coordinator and get directly to the Program Director of the agency. He promptly (this took about six weeks) set up a parent/child interview. Without the child, of course, for one does not want to form any false first impressions, does one?

Still, progress.

The Program Director agreed that there was an obvious problem and the parent was acting wisely in seeking services. "However, our Agency doesn't specifically serve your child's age group," or "Your child tests too high/low (underline one) and you should go, etc." So they go, either dragging the kid to be interviewed again, or getting sitters.

If the parent is *cunning*, when referred to the next agency, she will find out in advance exactly what the referred agency requires and conform to it, even though it may serve a completely different problem. That way the child will be accepted, the parent has more time to explore further, and the staff gets a new challenge.

To digress for a moment. A lot of people are startled at the fact that there is a pecking order in the handicapped world. Some parents will joyously embrace a diagnosis of Emotionally Disturbed or Autism rather than Retardation. One woman preferred to say her child was aphasic rather than say he couldn't talk. Higher-testing handicapped persons are separated from lower ones. Some agencies wouldn't dream of serving a handicap who couldn't be "cured." Children will be taken out of programs and classes if they don't conform to some rating scale established ten years earlier.

I find this status thing understandable but annoying because it is the handicapped who suffer in the long run. I can get "emotionally disturbed" over the diagnosis Emotionally Disturbed because it is a timed bomb that can explode and send shrapnel in all directions. Another pet peeve of mine is the big push to get kids into higher-testing type programs, often putting them in stressful competitive situations. I'll go into this more in the chapter on Special Education.

Without trying to sound light hearted, a multi-handicapped diagnosis can have some advantages. One can fit into several different agencies. Sound jaded? One can become jaded in this field.

Fast.

Okay, now the parent has found a program or service. Complacency sets in. After all that effort the parent feels the relaxation of accomplishment.

Watch it!

Any number of fast-acting things can happen:

    The place goes broke;

    The new director has a new philosophy and decides to employ only staff (no clients) as they are easier to control, if properly motivated;

    The Agency's budget is reduced and your program is cut because the parents sitting on the Board want the monies for the program their kids are in;

    The Living Legend at the helm of the Agency becomes the late Living Legend and no one person has the courage to assume the helm and the place goes under;

    A Federal, State, or County committee decides to re-channel funds into a new, badly needed sports complex and there goes your agency's funding.

The watchwords might be: *You get a program for your handicapped child and you watch it like a hawk.*

Otherwise parents may well find themselves, one glorious day, with egg on their faces and their child back in front of the TV.

There is a very real bind in which parents find themselves. I'll try to rephrase a rather crude aerospace-ism to explain. You are up to your nose in professional "effluence" and you holler, "Please, don't make any waves!" Parents are trapped in sort of a blackmailed position. If they are too obstreperous the kid can get cut out of a school or program right now, saddled with a damning record and it's bye-bye services. I'll protect the innocent here and not get too specific, but the stories of parents who have been ostracized for "making waves" are hair raising. To raise hell can put you in a position of fear, believe me. It is better to swap causes. Let someone else fight your battles; someone who doesn't have any direct stake. You can reciprocate when they are being threatened. The best way is to let the professionals do your fighting for you. To see professionals infighting can be as engrossing as any aerial dogfight the Red Baron ever put on.

Chapter Four
Social Workers

When you are pregnant you select an obstretician. When the baby arrives, you likewise select a pediatrician. But when you have a handicapped child you somewhere along the line get (notice I didn't say *select*) a Social Worker.

In lieu of a satisfactory dictionary definition of a Social Worker, someone suggested that I give a lucid, humorous description.

I can't. Social Workers are human beings subject to the same vagaries of life that the rest of us lesser mortals are. Social Workers are tall, short, thin, heavy, come in all colors of each sex, and vary widely in effectiveness. Some are quite likeable, others are gross. Again, they are human beings.

If you have never been assigned a Social Worker, skip this chapter and move briskly to Religion. On second thought, stick around; you might learn something that will be useful in the future.

I'll never forget my first interview with a Social Worker (not counting the Intake Worker, whom I figured as an importantly titled clerk).

At that time, my personal life had taken a busy turn for the worst. In less than six months my child had been diagnosed as handicapped, my new baby had a birthmark which we considered cosmic, my mother died (across the country) and two weeks later I had major surgery. My father died a month after my mother, leaving us responsible for a 16-year-old brother and a 19-year-old sister. Somehow all this got settled and I glanced at my calendar to see what other wonder was in store for me. I discovered I had scheduled my first in-depth interview with a Social Worker. Why not? After countless meetings with lawyers, undertakers, and travel agents, certainly a Social Worker couldn't be any more peculiar.

As usual, I was wrong.

I arrived at the scheduled time, snappily attired in my best wash-and-wear, Pablum-colored house uniform (new baby, remember), with suitably aged sneakers on my feet, one leg shaved and not a care in the world. I found a place to park outside a building that was painted Advanced Gangreen, and proceeded through the puddles of rain into a converted Quonset hut. There I encountered the volunteer receptionist. When she was confronted with this apparition (me) she went into shock. I then was beckoned (she probably thought the spoken word would have me re-mounting my broom or casting evil spells) to a bench where there was the usual captivating literature. You know the stuff. "Your Damaged Child Need Not Be An

Abandoned Soul," and the usual dogeared digest with the inevitable condensed article on how to be a successful career mother while being lovely, desirable, and sexually stimulating to your spouse in ten days or less. Fortunately, I had my check book with me and could add and subtract what this visit would cost us if the kid had any long-term problems. While waiting I looked at my fellow sufferers and noticed we all avoided direct eye contact. Some mothers had their kids with them and they were really having a time. One poor woman had her charming child putting on a stellar performance. You name it and he was doing it. The mother was dressed smartly and was trying valiantly to maintain some dignity, but when the little rotter emptied the contents of her purse all over the reception room she gave in and burst into tears. You could hear the receptionist give an audible sniff of disapproval, which gave a nice dimension to this pocket tragedy.

Being more appropriately dressed for a floor scramble, I tried to help the mother get all her belongings together. Neither of us spoke or looked at each other. Suddenly, I became aware of this person standing next to me. Actually, all I could see were two legs and sensible, but stylish, shoes. After all the stuff was retrieved I got up (and up and up and up) to look into the face of this elegantly turned-out person who was watching us with absolutely *no* expression. What I had at first perceived to be a store dummy finally asked if I was her nine o'clock appointment. I quickly checked my driver's license to remember my name, which I blurted out before I forgot it. It was conveyed to me that I should follow this humanoid.

I knew enough physics to know that sound doesn't

travel in a vacuum, so I felt I must test the atmosphere and started babbling something about the poor woman in the lobby, etc. Apparently, whatever I said was very profound, for the robot stopped immediately and spoke. Egad. Not only did she speak, but a pencil was whipped out and stood readily over a pad while the robot intoned, "That's interesting. Would you tell me *why* you care about the woman in the lobby?" I had been asked so many dumb questions in the past few months, what with one thing and another, that I didn't find her question unusual. I don't remember my answer, but I know it was recorded for posterity in her little tablet.

There followed a scene only an overtrained professional can stage manage. When we entered her office (with me trailing as due my inferior role), the door was firmly closed and my Social Worker sat down behind her desk in her Executive Swivel Chair. At first I thought I had been forgotten. What seemed like hours went by as she perused an impressive file, while I stood there like a lump, my shoes pointed inward, and I fought an overwhelming urge to whistle or hum. I also should mention that I was using a diaper bag for a purse, as I had to take the baby to the pediatrician later that day.

The office was shoe-box shaped and not much bigger. My razor-sharp mind told me that there was no chair for me and I realized immediately that we were going to have quite an informal session, with me either on the floor (as in Girl Scouts) or perched on her desk (as at the office Xmas party).

At last this deity seemed to decide that my hulking, looming mass was distracting her from her homework, and she motioned me to an area to the left of her desk, where I obediently stood. Finally, she told me I could sit down. I thought that was very thoughtful of her, but I couldn't find anything to set my considerable bulk on without courting disaster (by then I had discovered what appeared to be a doll chair next to her desk). But yes, by God, *yes.* The "doll chair" was MY chair. You've all seen those *National Geographic* photographs showing the Aborigines squatting with their knees under their chins, staring blankly ahead. You now have the picture of my posture. The only thing that even barely saved my dignity was that skirts were somewhat longer in those days. It was going to be a long fifty minutes.

She got a little miffy when I suggested that all the questions about my youth could have been gotten far more easily from my school yearbooks.

Curiously enough, I don't recall her asking anything about my then present state of affairs, to say nothing about my handicapped child. But then there are some things I will never understand.

Sometime later I was left alone briefly with my file and quickly read the report of the interview. I'm glad I don't have an identify crisis. From that experience I learned a new trick — it's called "negative adaptation.*

People react differently to interviews with Social Workers. Some emerge from initial interviews looking quite satisfied. Others are traumatized into psychoses. One man who read a lot was able to get a fairly normal

---

*"Negative adaptation" is the ability to ignore your surroundings. It can be useful in many ways.

interview because he had read *The Organization Man* and knew he had to love his father more than his mother in order to appear adjusted. His wife didn't do as well. She (the dumb chick) was told to be "honest and straightforward." She was. Her case history is being used as required reading for Sociology 1A. On the post-graduate level, she personally is brought in for study. A teal textbook case. A good example of a reasonably nice, bewildered woman undergoing therapy she didn't know she needed.

Women always seem to come off worse in these interviews or group sessions. Whether it is a case of mothers being more available than fathers, thereby getting more exposure, or whether the whole system is male dominated, and we are looking at Machismo, is open for debate. I'll leave it up to you to decide. I just wanted to throw in a little Women's Lib to keep you all from snoozing too deeply.

Some people will do anything to get out of seeing their Social Worker. One particular day I didn't feel up to seeing mine. So when I saw her coming I crawled under a table and told my staff to tell her they didn't know where I was. But they were spared having to lie because she spotted me immediately and zeroed in. She was the kind of Social Worker who expected her cases to be sitting under tables. I thought fast, put my finger to my lips and whispered, "Shhh, we're teaching the children a therapeutic adaptive activity." (Now there isn't a professional living who would interrupt *anything* "therapeutic" and "adaptive.") She thoughtfully tip-toed out of the room and fortunately didn't look back or she would have seen a room full of people lying on the floor, apparently having a mass seizure.

My present Social Workers (I get them assigned in teams or squads) are all a little "antsy" since I announced that I am writing a book and a whole chapter will be devoted to Social Workers.

However, in order not to seem biased, the author will report in this chapter experiences of others regarding "What to do about Social Workers."

One highly articulate person I know has been reduced to writing her Social Worker, which is the only way she can hope that her statements won't be misinterpreted due to voice tone, facial expression, dress style, and other assorted "significant" body twitches.

One unfortunate neophyte walked into his "Intake Social Worker" interview and was greeted with the professionally stereotyped sentence, "You must feel guilty today." The parent apologized profusely, saying that the traffic was heavy and he was sorry that he was twelve seconds late for the interview. Wrong answer. He was told that he should be feeling guilty because he had a handicapped child. (See chapter on "Guilt.") Puzzlement all around.

"Guilt" is writ large in handicaps. Are you "guilty" about anything, reader?

Some strange things can crop up in well-meaning, zealously applied theories. There is a movement afoot called "Normalization" for the handicapped, meaning that a handicapped person is entitled to the same opportunities, benefits, and rights, as anyone else. However, the fly in the ointment seems to be in reaching agreement on the definition of "normal." One speaker said his dictionary defined "normal" as "Perpendicular at right angles," which may give you some idea of the problems.

I once heard a professor in a Health course say that in health statistical circles it was considered "normal" for a large percentage of Egyptians to have blood in the urine due to a high incidence of a parasite known as shishtotamyosis. It was also "normal" for Americans to have a high incidence of respiratory infections, and for the Eskimos to have cancer. I found myself wondering if anyone had ever done a rating scale on the "normalcy" of college professors. (An informed source on Public Health tells me that the professor meant "norms," which is something completely different; he probably figured no one was listening to him anyway, since it was a "required" course.)

I recently listened in bemused wonder to a group discussing a Social Worker's gung-ho idea that patients in State Hospitals for the mentally retarded should be allowed to exercise their right to vote. With great dedication he carefully tutored them on the process, and they were duly registered and voted. The group was discussing this feat of "normalcy" with amazement because it was an especially complicated ballot, which most of us didn't understand, and we weren't in a State Hospital for the mentally retarded. Carrying this to its logical conclusion, we know that all registered voters are eligible for jury duty and await with interest the moment the lawyers and judge in that county are faced with "Civil Rights" and "Normalization."

In a similar vein, I heard a story from the mother of a multi-handicapped boy who had been ordered to report for the draft shortly before his 18th birthday. And when I say multi-handicapped, I mean there wasn't an inch of this boy that didn't have a problem area. The letter arrived ordering him to register personally for the draft. The family naturally thought the computer had short circuited and they wrote a letter explaining why it would be impossible for the boy to show up in person. To their disbelief, they got a really rough letter with barely veiled hints of jail, or worse (public flogging?) if this young man did not report to his draft board immediately. It somehow got resolved and the family was spared the public humiliation of their son.

A group of us were rapping about what we would have done in the same situation and I must freely admit that we shouldn't be allowed loose. One woman said that she would have painstakingly taught the kid to salute and then delivered him directly to the letter writer — sparing the local draft board. Her faulty thinking was pointed out to her, because the letter writer was probably a computer named Hal and also did the work for the regional mailing lists for magazine subscriptions.

One timid, mousy-looking member then told us what she actually DID. All smiles, she took her son down to the draft board and announced to the bewildered chap at the desk, "We are so happy! Here's George and his packed luggage plus your letter and you don't know how much future planning you have saved us. And not only that, the military is saving the government MONEY. Now we don't have to apply for ATD (Aid to Totally Dependent)." The situation was cleared up with supersonic speed, even though poor George was puzzled at having to unpack without going anywhere. That mother has to be *watched.*

In browsing through the textbooks, it is a miracle that all Social Workers don't apply for hazard pay, especially if they follow some of the advice I have read on counseling parents. I particularly liked the line, "Let the parents feel they are making the decision so the counselor won't be blamed later if it doesn't work out." Okay, yell "Out of Context." See if I care.

In order not to imply that all Social Workers are ogres, incompetent, or mentally handicapped themselves, let us consider some neat examples of outstanding individuals.

A couple who was placing their beloved, very young child away from home had a scheduled interview with the DREADED SOCIAL WORKER! Tension all around. Mother looked defensive and close mouthed. Father looked torn with sorrow and constipated with reluctance. Enter Social Worker — a very lovely, alert-looking young woman. First question: "Tell me all about your child." No laying on of "Guilt," or "What position was the child conceived in?" — but "Tell me about your child." It saved *that* interview.

Another woman was in the solitary position of hell raising at a board meeting. The meeting was hostile; she was alone in her rage and it was a grueling hard drive. She created a considerable scene, and then discovered her Social Worker in the audience! Says she, "Wow, that is what I call doing a good job." The parent recommended an immediate raise for the Social Worker.

The most hilarious interview that I've heard about involved two parents assembled in their own lovely living room with their newly acquired Social Worker. They were serving an elegant deli lunch, with an appropriate wine, and settling down for a cozy interview. The mother had been warned to keep her mouth shut and be eyeball cued by her husband. The father assumed the physical posture of the successful executive (which he was), blended with a nice look of cooperation, although slightly tempered with a no-nonsense look on his face. The $2000.00 stereo equipment had suitable Social Worker Interview Mit Lunch music murmuring in the background. The stage had been set.

Apparently the Social Worker was used to such interviews; her opening statement was: "You people in this area turn interviews into social events, rather than serious interviews." This did happen to be a high-income/education suburb. It was a little difficult for the worker to do her job. At each pertinent comment that was made, she had to put her lap lunch down in order to take notes. Since no respectable Social Worker would drink during an interview, she was disconcerted at having to cope with aside comments about the wine being young-but-not-pretentious type of thing. Both parents did notice that she kept glancing rather puzzedly upward. That mystery was solved later for the parents, never for the Social Worker. There was a rubber chicken hung in the floor-to-ceiling drapes, left over from a 40th birthday party the weekend before. From a short distance it looked *very* realistic. Since then the Social Worker has gone into marriage counseling. After she got her divorce.

There are extremes in this field, and one can cite examples from both sides. On the negative pole we have the guy who was told his Social Worker had committed suicide. An announcement that filled him with a feeling of warm satisfaction. Another maladjusted parent refused her Social Worker's recommendation for "heavy" therapy on the grounds that the Social Worker weighed two hundred pounds and perhaps was in need of some therapy herself.

On the positive side there was the Social Worker who fought long and hard for parents to acquire a badly needed service for their children. I will implicitly trust the advice and judgment of a person who has always been accurate, honest, and informed. And even more important, one who is genuinely concerned about the welfare of the child. That is what it's all about. Or should be.

Also remember that frequently if the parent comes across as weird enough, the Social Worker will have a great deal of sympathy for the child and you will obtain the necessary services.

Social Worker interviews might be equated with baldness and menstrual cycles — an existing fact that cannot be altered, so must be borne. Gracefully, if possible.

Chapter Five
Special Education

I met Special Ed (as we insiders call it) in the form of a big, shaggy, bear-like man. I had found out there was an opening in the new school for one child. And I knew one child who qualified. At what seems to this day like Mach 5 speed I got an appointment with him.

My child patiently sat through the forty pages of questions I had to answer (we both had done this drill before) and again, it was duly noted that I quit nursing the kid because I was tired of wearing things that buttoned down the front, etc. At the conclusion of the session, the principal stood up, smiled at both of us, and said, "We'll see you Monday." I thought, Ech, another interview, and said, "What time do you want to see us?" He seemed startled and quickly consulted his notes. He then turned to me directly and said, "Why, I thought you said your child wouldn't mind riding with strangers and the school bus will be at your door to go to school Monday."

I reacted quite rationally.

I merely burst into tears, threw my arms around the principal, gave him and my kid a big kiss, resisted the impulse to do a handspring, raced home, got my husband out of an important meeting, opened the anniversary champagne, called all my friends and some of my enemies, hauled out the filet and wild rice, polished the silver, put the kids to bed for the night, and got all glamorous for a festive dinner with candles — the jubilant scene. The fact that it was only 3 p.m. didn't dampen my enthusiasm.

The principal told me later that with my positive attitude I was going to learn a lot. He was quite correct.

Entering the world of Special Education is much like going to a foreign country where an obscure language is spoken. Just as you get used to the language and can understand one out of every five sentences the teacher says, they up and change the whole concept and you are left with an obsolete vocabulary. I find myself frequently saying, "Whazzat mean?" So now I take a friend who is a special ed teacher when I go looking at programs. That way when someone tells me something that sounds like they are teaching a certain child that his fine motor muscle, spacial perceptive activity is socially regressive and countraproductive to peer-superior acceptance, my interpreter whispers to me that they are teaching the kid not to pick his nose in public.

An outstanding program can cause wonder and adulation and with good reason. A quirky little example may shed some light. A family suddenly noticed a *big* change in their child's attitude about catching the school bus. This child didn't talk, but her attitudes were observable to the parents. The mother used to be an executive secretary and had learned non-verbal forms of communication and the father knew a happy face when it beamed upon him.

Well, one afternoon, this precious one popped off the bus all giggly and stimulated, with much unintelligible but obviously positive arm waving. Good ol' Mom checks to see if there is a new driver. Nope. Oh, well, maybe it was just a good day.

This bus scenario was repeated daily. Happy, enthusiastic child eager to get to school and if asked about her day was able to convey a solar radiance. After about a week of this, the mother sent in some of her prize roses with a note saying, "Dear Mrs. G., Whatever you're doing, keep it up! Bonnie is positively aglow with enthusiasm. We've never seen her so happy." That afternoon the child came home with a note pinned to the back of her dress (didn't know it was there so couldn't chew it up) saying, "Dear Mrs. D., I'm Bonnie's new teacher and we're having a good time. I figured the roses were for me and I am enjoying them. Thank you. Mrs. H." Mother flew down to the school, full sail: "Where and who is Mrs. H?"

God love the Mr., Mrs., Ms. H's of Special Ed. These are the innovative, imaginative persons who can make or break your child's success. Generally, they are also too busy to be seeking self-aggrandizement.

Watch out for snow job artists who are impressive at first and know how to play the "professional" role to the hilt.

It is a sad fact that a good program can be dependent

on personality. I've seen outstanding people let go into oblivion because most parents don't realize this simple equation:

$$GP = I^3 \times \frac{HW^4}{R^2} + S^\infty$$

Good program equals initiative, inventiveness, imagination times hard work to the 4th power, divided by reality and resources plus support to infinity.

This brings us to the unsung heros and heroines of Special Ed — the Aides, sometimes called, "Paraprofessionals." An Aide's job is to assist the teacher in carrying out the teacher's curriculum. Often, the Aide is the most effective member of the team. I've been in schools where the policy was that the Aide should be seen and not heard, even though the Aide may be "carrying" the teacher, including drawing up class plans. I know firsthand about that. I was embarking on an unfamiliar venture and it was a teacher's Aide who kept me from falling on my face during the first year. Several times this Aide stopped me before I wandered out on the thin ice. But guess who got the credit?

Your child can be assigned a school that can either be a bustling hive of productive activities where the students learn computer programming, the PTA meets daily, the staff work together with mutual respect, the principal is a serene individual who is forward thinking and *au courrant* with present trends and the janitor keeps the place sparkling clean.

Or it could be a place like good old Happy Hollow Handicapped Haven, where the atmosphere is one of contained chaos. The teachers close off their classrooms and pull the shades. The Aides are treated like inmates and made to eat at separate times and places. The school nurse is paranoid. The principal is afraid of children. The janitor is a slob, and the staff dog is hostile. The parents have gone underground and the PTA doesn't meet because no one has assumed leadership. Staff turnover is unbelievable until you learn the situation.

Special Ed has as many ways of operating as there are school districts. Families have been known to move just to be near a reportedly fine program only to find that the principal and staff have all just resigned over a dispute about the kind of furniture that should be in the teachers' lounge.

There are two schools of thought in Special Ed, if you like puns (or even if you don't). One is "academically oriented," and the other is "task oriented." What does that mean? Academically oriented means the three Rs. Task oriented means learning how to survive without books — things like cooking, housework, yardwork, work work — that sort of thing.

Parents are responsible for keeping the fires of discussion burning brightly. We all want the goals for our children to be the highest. The "highest" is to have your child reinventing the light bulb and modifying the entire electronics industry. From pre-school on, the children are exposed to things that weren't dreamed of ten years ago. I was so shocked to have my second grader tell me about

Jovial planets that I was tempted to ask him to write a term paper for an astronomy class I was taking at the time. When *I* was in second grade we saw movies of the local bakery.

In Special Ed there reigns the eternal discussion, what will the child learn? How to come in out of the rain or how to translate Homer in the original while testing under 80. I will come out here and say I am "task oriented," so that you will know my position and we can argue like civilized savages.

I am all for *everyone* learning how to make beds, do dishes, cook, clean, garden, groom pets, wash clothes, iron, count out money, set the table, clear the table, build cabinets, saw wood, prune trees — you know what I mean. In other words, all the talents that the military, being single, being married, and life require to get with it.

The rub seems to be that some parents feel that their child is never going to be someone's servant. That is right, and I agree. But nevertheless, I think it is unrealistic to expect the handicapped to be so devoid of job skills that they cannot blow their noses without the help of the staff.

Enjoying simple skills is perfectly acceptable. I know a man who is very brilliant and creates engineering masterpieces with boring regularity. Of which of his projects is he the most proud? His intricately laid-out brick patio. I personally find much satisfaction from clearing our mountain lot and limbing trees with a long-handled, doubled-edged ax, which I do quite professionally, incidentally. You don't have to test very high to master the rhythm. You *do* have to put up with such random lines as, "Stay out of the way when your mother is using the ax." Or,

"Hey, fella, if I had a wife who could use one of those things like that I would be reeeeal careful." But that is a minor consideration when you realize the therapy of naming each branch after a pet gripe and raising that finely honed ax over your head and letting go. A friend has the most beautiful rose garden in existence. I found out that it is therapy for him to prune the hell out of the bushes, kill all those wee beasties that love roses, and spray endlessly for the myriad afflictions of roses.

These are *accomplishments* and they are *satisfying*.

One day we were short staffed on our handicapped program and told the students to help us do the dishes. We found to our amazement that with supervision (got to watch that soap!) they all had a ball. They were doing what the staff did, and thought it was a big deal. From then on, we shamelessly put 'em to work on everything. If it was good enough for the staff, it was good enough for the students. We all benefited.

I visited a TMR school where I saw someone doing ironing that put me to shame (my kids are culturally deprived as they have never seen me near an iron). Another class was busily making soup which they sold and used the money for the student body fund. The ceramics department sounded interesting and I condescendingly decided to look it over. I discovered a truly beautiful vase, hinted that I would like it and inquired about the price. The price seemed rather hefty, and anyway it was contracted out to a world-famous store as were other wares. There I stood, bemused out of my mind that these wonders were produced by persons testing very low.

If you seek further humilation, go to a sheltered

workshop some day and try to do some of the jobs there. This reminds me of something I overheard on a sheltered workshop tour. This mother said she had never considered workshops as she wanted her son to have a "normal" childhood. When I asked someone how old the child was, I found out he was a huge, surly Downs kid who was twelve. Good luck, Mother. Time does have a way of getting away from one.

Task-oriented education has a practical side. I think one can learn to count and read just as well by, say, here are six shirts, four handkerchiefs, twelve red chessmen, twelve white chessmen, with round, felt bases on twelve black squares at $75.00 a set, packed in four pounds of styrofoam and shipped by surface transportation for 3¢ a pound, while we make our balanced lunch of protein, fruit, and carbohydrates, with a sharp knife to cut it and then sit down to eat it under the walnut tree that we harvested last fall, and husked and sold the nuts for $1.25 (less than the store) and watered Mrs. White's begonia bed with soft water, killing the entire thing (nobody's perfect).

I will never forget this line I once overheard. Here is this adult standing there waiting patiently to be served (he lived at home with capable parents) and this new staff type said, "What's this? You're handicapped, not helpless. Serve yourself!" A new era was introduced. *Everyone* can do *something*. It just takes imagination.

Mail all your complaints about the above to your Social Worker.

I mentioned status in an earlier chapter and want to bring it up again here. This is a fiercely competitive environment we all live in. If you don't believe me, go to a

Little League game and tape record the grandstand "advice" or watch a boxing match on TV with the sound turned off. One kid I know came tearing home and asked his mom if he had ever had any stitches. When Mother wanted to know why he was interested she found that his seatmate at school had had an appalling number darned on him and this kid didn't want to be left out of the race. Any baby shower will turn up the "Can You Top This" game of difficult labors and episiotomy stitching. A classroom situation is no different — as a matter of fact, it's worse because this is the training ground for the rest of life.

In Special Ed school systems there are all levels of classes and a depressing number of parents pushing for their kids to achieve the highest category and consider it the epitome of the parents' "success" when they get their child in a "normal" class. One mother admitted to me that she single-handedly got her daughter through high school and into a good job. The daughter is now working and is unhappy. In this headlong pursuit of the diploma, the fact that the child was being trained in a life style she could never achieve was overlooked. Now the girl is lonesome, aware of her inadequacies, but unable to do anything about it and is isolated from her peers. I am not advocating letting the child go on without stimulation to do better. I am advocating realism. I am advocating thought about what the daily exposure to having practically the whole school smarter than you and knowing it. And knowing the whole school knows it. Being low man on the totem pole constantly can be crushing.

Our entire staff found out that the kids who tested

highest required more of our leisure time activities than the others. These children were under the dual stress of being academically pushed on one side and parentally pushed on the other. Our order of the day was, "Get off their backs," and then we saw all kinds of blooming. No one is comfortable out of his element his whole life. I recall with deep pain a spiritually beautiful youngster who was multi-racial, physically perfect, mentally cheerful and mortally isolated. We all remember the glow that he would get when he came to us. We can still see the dazzling pride on his face when he got a gold medal at the Special Olympics. I can still feel the warm, sturdy hug I got from him after I had chewed out his parents for pushing him too hard.

He's gone.

He wasn't "smart" enough and it embarrassed his parents that we had quietly changed him from a room-hidden introvert to an award-winning achiever with buddies — real buddies — the kind you fight with, the kind who cheer you on, the kind where you feel bad if they get hurt or sick. I am talking about the kind of buddy who won't call you "stupid" or reject your overtures of companionship.

I know you're out there, big man, and I hope it isn't too awfully lonesome.

I know one kid whom I adore for a variety of reasons, none applying to reality. His language is truly appalling. We never discouraged him because we regarded this trait as a superior form of communication. He was a natural mechanic and could repair bikes, door latches, thread movie projectors, etc. Well, he had built up a reservoir of contempt for a particular teacher (something he shared with a large group). One day this teacher told him to do something unreasonable and the kid let loose with two words, one of which is that popular four-letter Anglo Saxonism beginning with "f." It was said with great sincerity. The teacher turned to me with absolute shock and said, "How terrible! This child shouldn't be in this school." With Herculean effort I was able to contain myself long enough to agree — the kid should be in a higher level class situation. He had used the expression at exactly the right time and place and in the right situation.

I strongly feel that no parent should criticize any program until that parent has personally spent several hours *working* in the school with the teachers, and has gone on at least one field trip.

Field trips are not like ego trips, incidentally. They are more like drug trips — a real nightmare. The kids love them. A bond of respect is built up between the teachers and volunteers as results of field trips — similar to the bond of respect that troops in the trenches build up. One spends a lot of time in or near the bathrooms. Continuous head counts are made, but that doesn't prevent the hair-raising moment when someone discovers that no one has seen Mary for awhile. Mary has decided it would be fun to join the sharks in their tank and the attendants are having trouble talking her out of it. Explaining what happened to Mary's mother takes rare talent.

I personally got my education in Special Ed with handicapped persons when I was ordered to help out on a summer school session. I came through with a towering admiration for the staff and an appreciation of the needs of the students.

It was that summer also that I saw how thoughtless the public can be toward handicapped persons. On our outings we were stared at, shied away from, commented on and actually rejected in some instances. One day a group of tourists took moving pictures of our group and they should really have a dilly of a film. The staff hid all of the participants behind them and then proceeded to act rather irrationally. I let this insanity continue as I felt that it would spruce up home movies somewhere.

I found myself becoming fiercely protective toward all people subjected to this kind of exposure. One especially bad scene should show you what I mean. We were having a beautiful picnic at a nice park when we became aware that a lot of people were staring at us as we lined up at the train ride. One pregnant woman tried to shield her children and said that our children shouldn't be allowed in public. She said this loudly. The children all heard it as did the rest of the people there. No one spoke up against her attitude, and that so incensed the kindly bus driver that he walked up to the woman and in a clear, loud tone said, "Madam, I would suggest you go home and pray that the child you are carrying is perfect." At this point we all broke into cheers and applause. The kids love to cheer.

This public rejection, however, can be used to the advantage of the handicapped. I know one parent who is always able to get the best seats in the house, be first on the rides, have the most cleared area, the best picnic benches, the entire playground — anything the group wants. When asked for the secret to these successes, the parent finally admitted to getting an important, solemn expression, going in advance of the group and saying significantly in tones of doom, "There is a school for cripples coming here."

It never fails because everyone knows handicaps are contagious. At least it appears that way sometimes.

The professionals are capable of thoughtlessness, too. One junior high teacher whose class was studying the brain got the bright idea to take his class on a tour of the school for the retarded. Everyone involved in the planning of that trip was wrong. The teacher learned something invaluable when one of his students got up in class later and quoted a person who had a tongue like a sword and the striking ability of an asp. "If you are studying the brain, you go to an autopsy."

One of my favorite principals gave in to a random impulse. As an expert in Special Education, he was asked to speak before a group of "gifted" children. He grew a bit weary of the aura of superiority present in the room so decided to throw out some food for thought. He told them they were fiscally considered under the same budgetary umbrella that the handicapped were. Since they were "gifted" children they all got the message.

Teacher-parent interviews are two-way streets, I guess. I was told this story, but think it could be just an "in" rumor. One mother was called in for an interview as her child couldn't be understood by anyone at school and they wished to discuss the matter. During the course of the interview, the mother got more and more bewildered as the report of her child's lack of communication took shape. When she said he always talked okay at home, they brought him in and he carried on a nice chat with his mother, who answered him in the same unintelligible way. The teacher pointed out that reinforcing the child's gibberish was bad for any hope for the future.

Tar Fu's mother was understandably miffed to find out that the teacher considered Chinese "gibberish." Mrs. Fu's confidence was thoroughly shaken when she discovered the fact that although the teacher knew Tar had a problem, she didn't realize the problem was that he was a Down's Syndrome child. Maybe it is a rumor, but it very well could be true.

I *am* for lots of parent-teacher conferences, though. Really, this is not a bizarre fetish on my part. This is a way a parent can find out what the student is doing and why. One parent quit spanking her child after she found out that at school the child was *told* to tear up all paper in tiny pieces to develop certain muscles. Another found out that the weird scenes her kid took up were imitations of the "class problem." You also learn if your child is TMR, EMR, EH, CP, or whatever.

If the reader isn't familiar with at least some of those initials, he is skipping around, didn't read Chapter Two, or is too far into the wrong book.

Chapter Six
My Sibling, the Savage

This chapter title came from a family who had just placed their oldest child in a residential home. They were very concerned about the effect this would have on their youngest child.

The situation had been explained in advance, and in great detail, to the younger child. The parents had decided that they would wait for the child to bring the matter up. Two long weeks went by and nothing from the kid — no questions, no comments — nothing. Here's a family that had, in essence, changed their entire life style and the damned kid wouldn't even mention it.

One day the child came out of his room and said, "Hey, Mom! Is Annie ever going to come back?"

Here it was. Mom stiffened her spine and hoped like the devil she was going to handle this right. She explained that Annie would come home for visits, but she would be living in her new home permanently. Mother then kept going on into one convoluted detail after another. Upon conclusion of this rather incoherent monologue the child looked her squarely in the eye and said, "In that case, can I have her kitty for my own?"

Mother reached for the cooking sherry rather than the child. But, upon reflection, it *did* open the dialogue.

Being the sibling of a handicapped brother or sister is a rough job. They see the time-consuming work and effort of both parents on behalf of this child. They see their sibling praised for something that everybody took for granted when they did it. "Big deal, he learned to button his coat; he *should*, he's 18."

Brothers and sisters often get stuck with the care of their slower family member. To their everloving credit most accept this responsibility with cooperation, often with grace. Family activities frequently are geared entirely around the ability and tolerances of the handicapped child. For example, one West Coast family told me that the duck pond was the *only* thing open on Christmas day. And let me tell you, a duck pond can get mighty dull.

There is an annual torture test that most parents undergo, which is attending their children's holiday programs. Fathers seem to suffer most in the yin-yang contrast of ability levels. They have never been room mothers and haven't developed a familiarity with these contrasts.

A kindergarten teacher told me that she asked one little girl where she was raised. The little girl promptly replied, "In a car pool." Her older brother was handicapped and the mother, daughter, and brother had spent a great deal of time in car pools going to and from therapy sessions, etc. That answer did serve to jolt the parents into realizing how narrow the sister's territory had been and arranged time exclusively for her, spoiling the kid rotten in the process, but why not?

When parents or families get respite from the responsibilities of the handicapped child, they frequently schedule a bewildering number of activities.

One small male got a bad report home from his teacher saying that he had told the class during "Share and Tell" that he was — the very next day — going to fly to Los Angeles; stay at a world-renowned resort; tour a full-scale mock-up of a new airplane; fly to Orange County where he was going to Disneyland; stay overnight with some swinging friends of his parents; rent a car and drive to San Diego where he would tour an aircraft carrier; and fly home four days later in a helicopter owned by a family friend. It seemed that Mom had forgotten to inform the teach that all this was *indeed* going to take place while their older child, who couldn't take the pace, was at Easter Seal Camp. The teacher finally understood. Sort of.

At a parent-teacher conference, the teacher was asked if the child ever mentioned any siblings. The teacher had thought the kid was an only child. Then the teacher learned that the child lived in constant fear that if he weren't "smart" enough he would be sent away from home like his sibling. If you think that shocked the teacher, imagine the impact on the parents when the child told them that one night during story time.

If the problem child is the last born it seems somewhat easier on the other family children. They will have established their niches, but not always. One woman admitted that she had married much too early just to escape the never-ending crises that always seemed to be happening at home because of an autistic little brother.

I heard a disturbing story which vividly illustrates some of the problems with which a family can be faced. A teacher/housewife decided she would like to make a little extra money on the side so took up private tutoring in her home. She, incidentally, had no experience, training, or exposure to the handicapped. One night one of her little students had a *grand mal* seizure during the lesson. What did this supposedly human teacher do? She put the child on the front porch and called the father to pick up his child *immediately*. Why did she take this humane course of action? She didn't want her own children to see such a disgusting thing as a seizure. The father was physically sick after he had administered the necessary aid to his ten-year-old daughter. All this took place in front of the family waiting in the car.

As any parent, teacher, or neighbor knows, one is never more humorous, or comic, or wise than when one is in the elementary grades. The wit is positively Olympian. On any given day you can see/hear outstanding examples of this wit. I was intrigued to learn that gales of laughter are invoked by the mere *mention* of "pantyhose." Thank goodness children are keeping current with "technology in everyday life" to get their kicks. There is also one traditional, old-fashioned stunt that never fails to bring them to their knees, and that is to stumble around in jerky motions, making twisted faces and hollering "M-R, M-R." To a child with a handicapped brother or sister this isn't too awfully funny. I wish they would replace it; or at least update it and holler "DD, DD" meaning Developmentally Disabled — a more current term.

One son watched his father turn to stone when two neighborhood children spat on his brain-damaged, beautiful sister, the spittle trailing down the pink cheek of this gentle, puzzled child who had come outside to do nothing more than to watch the other children play.

The children in the family suffer the same tensions, humiliations, stares, comments, taunts, rejections, frustrations, emotional fatigue, and other assorted aggravations that the parents undergo. To a more exquisite degree. They don't have the parental reinforcement of the handicapped child being their *own* flesh and blood.

The author views siblings with deep admiration.

All of which brings us to a sub-heading, which is as follows:

Maintaining Domestic Relationship

The ideal model family is one where the mother has time for her hobby which is designing hydraulic actuators; the father is successful and happy in his work; the house in the suburbs is spotless; the mountain cabin rings with the joyous shouts of the family during weekend visits; the children are well-adjusted individuals who love each other, especially their handicapped sibling; duties are assumed by all without being asked; the parents have total agreement and communication; the in-laws regularly entertain each other; the neighbors adore you, and you adore them; serenity glows from each domestic minute of the day.

In other words, a pipe dream.

I would like to share the following story with you, which gives a somewhat different dimension as to how things can be:

The cast of characters: Bill, the father; Mary, the mother; and David, a hyperactive six-year-old with no speech.

Bill, home from work in the late afternoon, would often take David to the city park so they could get some exercise, and Mary could get some rest.

The park had an enclosed track field with a neat unclimbable fence around it. Bill, being a big guy, could boost David over the fence where he would amuse himself by going through the bleachers, playing with the water fountains, throwing the sand around; in general, going over the whole place. Bill, who knew that David couldn't get out, was able to jog, or read a book, or contemplate the meaning of life in complete relaxation.

Bill, Mary, David and the neighborhood all benefited by this arrangement.

One memorable day, however, Dave got an independent thought. He didn't want to stay in the track field any longer. Since he couldn't talk, he fell back on the only way he knew to get immediate attention.

He started screaming and undressing.

Bill, who was used to this, loped over and peered at this familiar scene and decided to see if he could hold out longer than David.

As he was leaning against the fence he felt something on his arm and turned to face a group of agate-eyed policemen with weapons drawn, determination and disgust written on their faces. Bill's first rational thought was,

"Christ, I knew I was driving a little fast on the way to work this morning, but are they going to kill me for *that*?"

(Meanwhile, let's not forget David; by now completely naked, screaming, shaking the fence and in general looking pretty awful — dirt streaked, running nose, hysterical, torn clothes, the whole thing.)

Bill then learned that someone passing through the park had reported a child molestation taking place. This being a college town, the local police were well organized and had apprehended their man in a very short time.

So here stood this big, lovable father explaining that the kid was brain damaged and he was only seeing how long the tantrum could go on, and to call his wife Mary, who would explain everything, etc. All the while, David continued to provide a one-person Greek chorus of misery.

Mary got a call from the police captain who asked her to describe her child and his clothing because they thought they had caught a molester, but the child seemed to be unharmed, and so on. Mary got hold of herself and explained that Bill was indeed the child's step-father and, yes, the child was something of a problem, and to please send them both home now. The policemen immediately apologized to Bill — while driving him home with a silent and now clothed David.

Bill didn't speak to David for days, and you can believe that it was some time before ol' Dave got back to the park. The police regularly sent this award-winning father a sympathy card and he got the Bite-the-Bullet award from a parent's group.

It hardly seems necessary to say that having a handicapped child puts severe pressure loads on the bonds of matrimony.

Relatives

Ideally, the parents of a handicapped child should be orphaned with no brothers or sisters and the only known relatives living in another country who speak a language that no one wants to learn. This would eliminate a lot of perimeter complications.

Reader assignment: In your mind's eye think of what would happen if you were simply to announce to your relatives one day that, "We are going to build a mountain cabin and would like your advice on site, type, size, etc." You would, I think I can safely say, get as many opinions as you have relatives.

Announcing the fact that you have a handicapped child causes the same relative reaction. And during the holiday season Aunt Em and Uncle Fuzz will invariably announce that they have the only thirteen-year-old graduating magna cum laude from the Harvard Graduate School of Business. The fact that this whiz kid will probably be in the federal slammer by age twenty-one for price fixing is of little comfort.

But I too have relatives, as do my harrassed parents, so I am not going to tell war stories here.

How to Cope With Guilt

The only thing parents of a handicapped child should feel guilty about is the fact that they bought this book when they could have checked it out at the library for free.

Chapter Seven

Establishing Carpools and Other Traps

Parents of handicapped kids frequently get their first lesson on coping from carpools. Veteran carpoolers could be used by Highway Patrols to teach crises/tension driving skills to their officers.

There are some basic ground rules for setting up a good carpool. First, don't be too eager. Find out why Wilma Zilch is so anxious to start a pool. There is a good chance that Mrs. Zilch herself doesn't drive. After years of transporting little Sonny Zilch to various programs you will find yourself developing a bitter hatred for persons who don't know how to drive. Take the kid only on the condition that Mrs. Zilch will learn to drive within six weeks, or out she goes. Driving for non-drivers isn't even tax deductible.

You should personally inspect the car, determine the

emotional stability of the driver, the reliability of the turn takers, the auto insurance, the number of other children in the family also riding along, family pets and their propensity for car sickness, and the handicapped child. In that order.

If at all possible, do your own car maintenance. You will then be certain that the mechanic has your own best interests at heart. Carpooling is much like airplane flying; hours of tedium relieved by moments of sheer terror.

Avoid temptations of sloth. It looks great on paper to drive one week out of six — until it is your turn. Then you see your error. You are greeted with six persons, plus yourself (whom you forgot to count), one infant (yours), orthopedic appliances, a rotten cold, and the season's worst storm.

Discipline techniques are acquired from school bus drivers, kindergarten teachers, drill sergeants and specialists in the field of crowd control. Always use the seat belts. Other than the obvious safety factor, they also tend to keep the passengers where they belong. Having Hermia under the front seat tickling Georgie while David has a seizure on the back window ledge just as Tom rolls down the back window to make an obscene gesture he learned at school makes your carpool look unprofessional, if not downright weird.

If forceful tactics have to be used to restore discipline, there are many fine acceptable methods. One outstanding carpooler had only to use her voice. Normally she had a lovely, low-pitched, well-modulated speaking voice. It was often described as sexy. Well, she could stop entire lanes of traffic by yelling at some little darling who was out of line. Her voice could etch glass, cut diamonds, and could be heard for miles when she yelled. She didn't often have to repeat herself as even the deaf in the carpool got the message.

It looks better to the public if ordinary, everyday objects are used to quell disturbances (it is socially unacceptable behavior to beat up on handicapped kids with the usual child-beating devices). One of the most versatile is the plastic track seen in all homes where there are boys and little racing cars. It can be left on the dashboard without causing comment. It is long enough so that the entire carload of kids can be swatted without the driver having to turn around or take his eyes off the road. It is flexible and doesn't break or inflict anything more than a sting. Another very effective tool is the ubiquitous 39¢ thonged sandal. It can be simply removed from the foot and applied to a bottom in a trice.

There was some discussion about the long-handled wooden spoon. Very effective. But it tends to create strange traumas at home whenever mother gets one out to make a salad. That particular carpool will probably give some future shrinks years of income trying to figure out the reason for the big salad hangup. A fly swatter can also be used; in all areas and climes.

The ultimate weapon is as effective as it is brutal. It's The Threat. Deliver an obnoxious child home, march same to door — thin of lip and hard of eye — and announce to the parent that if this little darling doesn't shape up fast it's out of the carpool. Parental pressure will be exerted that night and you should have an amenable passenger the next time around.

When giving seat assignments, use judgment as to size, handicap, behavior, and health. It is disconcerting to the small, timid child to have a 180-pound seatmate have a seizure next to or on top of him. Also, the autistic child will resent being repeatedly undressed by the retarded kid who is learning self-care at school.

Never use food to subdue rebellions. First, it sets a pattern and you will soon regret the expense. Also, mothers at the end of the run will resent it for a variety of reasons, all of which you will hear about. Third, it makes a mess of the car. One car became so littered with cooky crumbs, popcorn, etc., that when it was taken in for service, the mechanic put the paper cover on the seat to protect *himself* from the mess, rather than the other way around. It was appropriately named The Cookie Car and the salesman who had sold it to the family probably wouldn't have recognized it.

The personalities of the drivers can have a real effect on the carpool. One exceptional carpool springs to mind. It thrived for years. All the drivers were eager to take their turns, the pick-ups and deliveries were happy, chatty occasions, the children never seemed to be naughty, all the drivers were elegantly groomed, the stay-at-homes were stunningly outfitted in lovely, clean robes, and the conversations were witty and stimulating. The ideal carpool. The fact that one of the drivers was a handsome senior airlines captain may have had something to do with its success.

If at all possible, spouses should share the fun of carpooling. It can be a rewarding learning experience. Fathers quite frequently get religion after mother has taken to her bed and he has to drive because there are no substitutes, for one contrived reason or another.

Former carpoolers tend to be disgustingly overemotional upon meeting again years later. Deep friendships evolve and can furnish hours of reminiscing. Entire meetings have come to a grinding halt when ex-drivers have met after separations caused by school buses.

One particularly disgraceful display of emotion came about when four drivers discovered each other at a funeral. There were shouts of joy, much embracing and comments on how much younger each looked and exchanges of anecdotes, such as the time the kid threw his labeled clothes out the window along with his life-sized body image drawing.

Since two of the ex-drivers were women and the other two men, all that display of affection raised many eyebrows. Little did the onlookers realize what a strong bond can grow when you have been a professional handicapped carpooler. They all look forward to that great reunion when they get to the big carpool in the sky.

"Did You Really Plan This!?"

> Consider the lilies of the field, how they grow; they toil not, neither do they spin. And yet I say unto you that even Solomon in all his glory was not arrayed like one of these.
> Matthew 6:28, 29

That's nice, but in our handicapped world there is no

place or time for lilies. The workers in this field operate at a flat-out pace with much wild humor. You say you didn't know there was any humor in handicaps? Humor is the underlying thread of sanity that runs throughout the fabric of this world.

This entire part will frankly be an Ode of Adoration to the parents, the handicapped, and the beautiful persons working with all of us.

Most of the hybrid humor and heroes come out of the programs and activities.

One story never fails to crack me up. Members of a recreation program were going out trick-or-treating. This was sort of an unusual outing and everyone was quite excited about it. The group had to go through a park that had its share of muggings, etc. The local newspaper was covering the event in depth.

The director, who is famous for heroic tensions, nervously called the police department to see if the group would be safe. The officer answering the call blandly assured the director that any group having twenty-five handicapped kids, forty adult volunteers, a reporter and photographer from the newspaper and a police dog named Fang would be ABSOLUTELY safe. Anywhere. Upon returning through the park, the group encountered a man who emerged from the shadows and asked what this group was. One of the more mouthy staff members answered, "We are retarded," to which the man replied he was psychotic; whereupon another free-spirited staff member invited him to be on the staff, since that was a prime qualification. The poor guy probably did get emotionally disturbed. He was a plainclothes police officer sent to keep a protective eye on the group.

Program directors, staff members and volunteers often view life through a different lens than their fellow companions in life.

One woman got to be known publicly as the "Mrs. Robinson of Retardation" because she decided that the children were around women too much. This female was shameless in recruiting males for her program. She pampered these warm bodies disgustingly, but was also able to get a cream-of-the-crop female staff due to this prime stable of males. One of the more perceptive males did admit that he had no end of chicks falling at his feet as a result of his work with the handicapped. They were all impressed when he told them what he did for these "poor, unfortunate, crippled, etc." The parents of these lovely young things trusted him implicitly because they thought that anyone who did that kind of work must be as pure as the driven snow, and so he appears. In addition, he is cheerful, hardworking and adorable. And I wouldn't trust him as far as I could throw him.

Speaking of being thrown, this same woman made the mistake of grabbing a kid in a full-blown temper tantrum. He was as strong as an ox and meaner than sin. The woman realized her mistake when she found herself in the top half of a full Immelman turn (in airplane talk that's an outside loop) and hollered, "Male staff!!" The guys mobilized immediately — one catching her bottom before it hit the deck — the other fielding the kid and sitting on him while awaiting mother. It was all done in the spirit of great good cheer. The kid was pinned to the exercise mat by a brace of males who gently subdued him while checking on each other's endurance.

In another program a volunteer made the idle remark that one child looked like Captain Kangaroo (it was that kind of a day). And guess what? He did. Everyone was so taken by this suggestion that they fell all over each other telling this to Mom at pickup time. After her initial shock, she agreed and the staff was delighted to see her capitalize on this by dressing him as Captain Kangaroo, to the mutual enjoyment of all. This same volunteer (who had a different approach to life) patiently taught one little kid a song. Now this may not appear as unusual — until you learn that the kid wouldn't say one word, not one word at all, but would sing, "Michael Rowed His Boat Ashore" for this volunteer. It drove the speech teacher back to school.

I am personally familiar with a program that must have had among the staff and volunteers the biggest collection of zany weirdos in existence. Anyone who didn't subscribe to their wild angle of approach didn't survive. During the first year the school's principal lost forty-six pounds and the janitor had a heart attack, forcing him into retirement (neither was *directly* related to the program). This group never stole; it was always moonlight expeditions to liberate material. They never lied; it was always broad mental reservations. They made Koolaid-scented candles for Xmas and their "Canine Therapist" was a thoroughbred Newfoundland "puppy" that weighed 125 lbs. and drank from the toilet bowl. They shook the parents by telling them that the kids were "painting their hang ups" as a class project. Parents finally learned that the project involved painting wooden coat hangers. They had a "jug" band that was about the funkiest sound in the area, and they body painted their children on swim day, giving the swim director apoplexy.

They were incapable of giving a straight answer — a gaggle of frustrated gag writers. An example of their Mother's Day project:

> "Dear Parents, friends, and others in the war zone:
>
> We tried heroically to think of something *Different* for Mother's Day, but found that all the sharp whips had us beaten hands down. So we have taken the "chicken stand" of DOING NOTHING in honor of Mother.
>
> This is nothing personal, believe us, but just a matter of facing the fact that the professionals can do a better job of honoring Mother. We will, however, kiss each darling and extend our wishes for a soothing day. Regards from the inept group of RECREATION.
>
> P.S. Some of us are mothers (believe it or not) and regard it as a signal victory to get through the day. Any day. Oh yes, this policy will be followed for Father's Day, too. Last year nobody knew what it was we sent home and it sort of hurt our feelings."

They loved their clients and this love was lavishly returned. The staff and volunteers were too dumb to know they "couldn't do it," so the kids were exposed to all sorts of projects. Some of these "projects" are etched on the brains of the parents and burnt in the hearts of the staff. They were the crosses in life to their direction and an irreverant source of irritation to their Board of Directors. Their jobs are constantly in jeopardy of cancellation. When asked to submit a program description they wrote, "Created, canonized, curtailed, contained, cut, and cancelled." It went over like a scat in the punchbowl.

On an exercise/recreation program a mother contributed to the nicknaming of one male staff member. This male, whom we will call Harry, didn't let anyone goof off just because he was handicapped, no sir! He kept everyone working vigorously and with little mercy. His main tool was his mouth. Wow, did Harry have mouth. One day a mother came to the door and asked that "that damned Harry" be introduced to her. This group had a lot of requests like that and the request was taken routinely, with Harry being summoned from the back forty for the introduction. This mother looked at him for a long time and then said she could see why her handicapped son always groused about "that damned Harry." Never just plain "Harry." From then on at roll he was addressed in that fashion and the kids picked up a new word to take home. Harry seemed rather proud of his new nickname.

A note of poignancy here. Harry belongs to a galaxy of bright, young stars whom I love as my own children. I hadn't seen Harry for about three months when he wandered in one day and gave me his usual, "Hi Chief, how's it going?" I wasn't really looking directly at him when I asked him how he was and he told me he was partially disabled. The lioness mother in me came into action. "What's this partial disability stuff?" Then I looked into Harry's face and he looked different. He told me he had gotten a severe viral infection during a recent epidemic and it had given him a sinus complication that impaired his hearing, paralyzed the side of his face and affected his speech. I waited until I got home to cry. Harry would be the *first* to tell me I shouldn't cry because it brings out my age. I found out later that this affliction hasn't stopped Harry from his wildly funny mode of life; he had told his boss that hiring the handicapped was a plus thing. Harry's problem illustrates what a thin line we all walk in life.

There is in existence a lifesize poster of a woman who has an expression like George Meany in drag with a caption reading, "Handicaps and Mental Health is a *Serious* Field."

My former staff dedicated their psychedelically painted warehouse the "GKS Memorial Chapel," complete with plaque.

Remember the zany weirdos I mentioned? Their leader greeted his new boss with the statement, "What do you want to hear about first — the memorial grove or the dog?" The look of complete baffled borderline hysteria that passed over the face of the new boss was delicious to observe.

This humor is contagious and its fallout is reflected on the handicapped. I've personally been responsible for turning docile, placid, quiet handicapped children into shouting, armwaving smartmouths. I get intense satisfaction each time I do it.

Sometime when you're not too busy, get on the staff of a summer day camp for the handicapped. Or volunteer for it, or visit it. Better yet, open your big mouth and offer to run it. It's on-the-job training for candidacy to Bedlam.

I have in my head a lifetime of memories of summer day camp. (All those crummy kites in the trees — all those human pyramids where the anchor men get so close to each other that questions are raised regarding staff morals, or trying to explain how you got a "Waffle Stomper" bruise on your bottom to your physician.) (Or why I hate lunchtime and rotate staff during, "Do *not* feed the staff dog your grapes, your mom wants you to have a balanced lunch," and that *doesn't* mean eating on the teeter totter.) (And, "Where is everybody?" and then finding "everybody" perched like a tree full of owls on the jungle gym, covered by a parachute, which would occasionally respond to a flick of wind revealing all sizes and shapes of legs.) (Or telling a kid his back isn't broken just because he fell off the fence, and besides, "Your mother forgot to write in emergency numbers and your doctor's name on your application form so we will just have to wing it and hope to bring off the situation" without law suits, seizures, or suicide.)

Chapter Eight
Special Stories, Special Olympics

    The participants in any program never cease to amaze and amuse their staffs. They are forever coming up with things no one expects that they knew or could do. Workers in our world often become crashing bores to "outsiders," as they are forever swapping experiences about, "Guess what so-and-so did today," and, "Wait until I tell you about my experiences there" type of thing.

    I once had an "autistic" child in my carpool. This little boy was so far out that even radar couldn't tell if he was a pulsar or a quasar. He didn't communicate or relate with *anything*. Everyone changed programs and I didn't see him for about five years until I ran into him one Saturday at a recreation program. He had grown up and the staff assured me he was still in another dimension, so I merely patted him on the head and told him I was glad to see him again. I was standing outside, talking to the director when I felt this soft, warm hand creep into mine. I looked down to see this "autistic" child all ready to go home with me in my new carpool. That shook me to my foundations, not to mention shaking up a lot of theories about that child.

One father told me how his low-testing daughter could always tell when the father was talking to an especial friend on the telephone without names being mentioned. It was eerie. Then the solution hit him. He used a different and apparently noticeable tone of voice and his daughter could always pick it up.

A much-admired teacher called a mother on some little item, and during the conversation, the mother mentioned that Julie had just opened the refrigerator and was busily mixing fruit color and water in a pitcher and the mother couldn't understand what had gotten into the child. The teacher explained that it was Julie's job in her classroom to mix the juice for snacks, and that probably the teacher's call had reminded her of this fun activity.

Do you know what the highest compliment is that you can pay any director of any handicapped program or service? Ask them who is handicapped and who is not. You didn't know that? Well, it's true.

There is a father wandering around, still mumbling to himself about something that had happened to him. He came into a program with his very small child and had *specific* directions on how to take care of the child. This was a loosely structured program with many activities going on at the same time, so Dad went up to a young man who was smiling at him and asked if the young man could help him. Sure enough, the young man explained he was a junior staff member. The father then launched into the litany of instructions for the care and feeding of his son — all of which was duly assimilated, understood, and agreed to. The director didn't interfere, as the young man, though handicapped, *was* quite capable of doing all those things. Dad was very impressed in the days that followed at how well his instructions were being adhered to. He suggested to the director that a promotion to full staff status was in order for our cooperative young man. Need I go further? The young man was later busted back to the ranks as he got heady with power and started disciplining.

Most of the general public are unaware of the fact that the handicapped are much better behaved than "normal" persons, because they *have* to be in order to get accepted. Once on a school shopping center tour, one blithe spirit was having the time of his life. He was singing, admiring everything, waving at everyone, skipping, humming, and dancing. A classmate couldn't stand it any longer. He came over to the blithe spirit and said, "For Heaven's sake, Alfredo; we're retarded, but we're not *that* retarded!"

Staffs and volunteers tend to have their little projects. One such staff was busily making a trophy to be awarded on bad days. The children were all involved in the design of it, too. There was one kid in a class for slow learners who seemed unusually taken with the project. And he also seemed to be remarkably well-informed. The project consisted of mounting a 40 mm shell on a wooden base to be declared the Super Bite the Bullet Award. Not too many people come in contact willingly with 40 mm shells, and here came the "slow learner" announcing, "Hmmmm, that sure is a neat 40 mm shell that's been fired experimentally because of the blue casing from a machine gun." The staff was going to ask him if he had the MILspec number, but decided he probably did, so settled upon asking him where he got his information. It seems this ordnance expert had a brother who was a gunner on a battleship, and he was familiar — obviously — with all kinds of shells. Incidentally, the trophy project turned out to be very obscene looking, so it remains hidden. It can be seen by appointment, however.

Yes, there is humor in our handicapped world. You still aren't convinced? Try these illustrations.

A recreation group was going on a walking tour to the local pizza parlor for samples, demonstrations, soft drinks, and old movies. The kids could barely sit still for roll call. A lot of these children never responded to any command; some had marginal toilet habits, some had traumatic aversions to bathrooms, and some were always wet or worse. After roll was taken, one consummate mother routinely announced, "Everyone to the bathroom before we go."

The ensuing scene left the staff standing in an empty room. All the kids had got up as one and were all in the johns vying with each other to be first. The girls weren't too bad, but the staff said that the scene in the boy's room was not to be believed. Incidentally, there wasn't one accident in the outing. A program first.

Bathrooms are big with our kids, so a lot of toilet humor evolves.

One summer day camp shared its premises with the county painters. These guys were patient when the kids got into their paint, or locked themselves in the paint truck, or were stolen blind by the staff of plastic sheeting and masking tape. In this particular day camp, there was a young man who loved to go to the bathroom, take off all his clothes, dip them and himself in the urinal and emerge naked as the proverbial jaybird. The kid had something of a problem. As he did this several times a day, the staff got a little weary of going to the john, retrieving his clothes and turning off the urinal. All the staff got stuck at one time or another, and so were developing a testy attitude about this kid.

One particularly trying day was slowly coming to an end. Everyone was closing down the facility, when someone heard a noise in the men's room, and our birthday-suit boy was nowhere to be seen. A very glamorous, leggy and upset female staff member kicked open the door of the john and yelled, "Get out of there this minute! I'm sick and tired of cleaning up after you!"

It was a county painter.

He admitted later to the convulsed staff that the incident shook him up for hours. The painters started using the teachers' bathroom as it had a lock on the door.

I can never forget the intrepid firefighters of Engine Company #4. When you are the director of a program operating out of a public school, many exciting things happen. I don't recommend it for the average neurotic. Well, anyway, we had 30 children, 10 staff members and approximately 10 volunteers. It was 4:49 p.m. on a dark, rainy evening and it was parent pick-up time. Parent pick-up time is when the smoothest tongued staff are put on door duty.

A shattering WAH WAH sound, rising and falling in pitch tore through the auditorium. What in God's name was that infernal racket? Five seconds later, two police cars and seven — count 'em — seven fire engines dripping with firemen fully dressed for a major disaster pulled up in front with sirens blaring. This fantastic, nightmarish scene greeted the now-arriving parents.

The door was flung open and in poured the biggest firemen I had ever seen. The kids were enchanted, the staff and volunteers were stunned, the parents were horrified, and the firemen were ready for action.

Some little darling had found the pretty red box that said, "Fire — Pull," and he did.

As this was a school, many companies automatically responded unless headed off. Since we weren't aware of the niceties of heading 'em off, there they were. Traffic was tied up for blocks and still the terrible alarm was wailing away. Finally Fireman Captain Jones decided which one was the director (the one with the red face) and asked if everything was all right. We figured out what had happened and all that remained to do was to handle it next time. The children all waved to the departing six engines and went home. The police straightened out the traffic, and the staff and volunteers disappeared into thin air. Nervous Nellie was left to take the rap.

Captain Jones had ginger curls peeking out from under his helmet, periwinkle blue eyes, and was *gigantic.* Also, his helmet talked to him, whereupon he would answer his pocket. *Each* time this happened, I would jump backward and *each* time would fall over another huge Smokey Stover wearing size 80 boots and a trench shovel in his belt, who would catch me and replace me in a standing position in front of Captain Jones again. If I hadn't been so embarrassed I would have enjoyed all that body contact.

He explained the procedure to me, which was useful information. The kids couldn't seem to leave that alarm alone, so the procedure arrived at was this: when the alarm was pulled the child was yelled at, the room emptied to 18 feet from the building, the runner sent to turn off the noise, another runner tear-assed out the front door, dashed to the street and waved the engine down (the firehouse was a half-block away), and then run like mad to the corner to meet the truck and they would call off the other six trucks before filling their reports. We met all *three* shifts of Engine #4, knew each other by first names and had such a warm rapport that they would routinely wave to us on their way back from fires.

One memorable occasion the alarm was pulled two days in a row at exactly the same time (to the minute). As I was racing out to the street for the first one, one of the firemen timed me and told me I was improving my form. The next day one of the staff asked why it took them longer to arrive than the previous day. It seemed they had washed the truck and were cruising around, drying it, and so had farther to come. (If the reader thinks I took these things lightly, I will explain that on the second day, I decided to let the staff learn first hand about being a director and hid myself with the participants and pretended to be seriously handicapped. The captain spotted me anyway and flashed me the peace sign.)

One little kid probably still goes around with his arm

permanently stuck in the alarm-pull position as I caught him at the moment of truth with my voice.

We solved the problem by putting up a huge STOP sign over the alarm and practiced a bit of negative reinforcement. Hasn't been pulled since, but I hear the group got back their prize puller so I expect to hear that the program and Engine Company #4 will have an opportunity for a reunion. I plan to miss it.

The Special Olympics

The Special Olympics are Olympic games held for the handicapped. They are as beneficial as fresh air. Unlike ordinary Olympians, Special Olympians *can* have medication. Naturally, the coaches, parents, and teachers want the best performances possible and will go to some lengths to achieve this end. One coach, aided and abetted by the parents, discovered a hyperactive boy who ran like a cheetah when he was off his tranquilizers. On the day of the races, guess who didn't get his medication? He won the 400-yard dash in record time. Since he didn't know or even care how far 400 yards were, a staff member was placed at the end to keep him from running into the next county. This same kid, incidentally, screamed like an eagle at the swim meet as he claimed they were shooting at him to get him to swim. A starter's gun can have that effect on some people. Our coach (a real sportsman) discovered that simple fact and got all his champs first, second, and third places in all events in which they were entered.

This coach was referred to by staff as Field Marshall Von Gerhardt because of his Prussian tactics on outings. On Olympic Day he had his staff deployed all over the field with whom he kept in touch by field phones. He got his staff on the field by the simple device of getting them all "official" badges. On checking with his top aide, he found out that Charlie had Males 10-12, while Ann was at the pool with Female Swimmers, 14 and over.

"What is Tom doing?" asked the field marshall. Silence on the other end of the field phone. "Repeat. What is Tom doing?"

"Tom has males, 8-10."

"How is he doing?" Another silence. "What is going on with males, 8-10?"

Top aide hesitated, then said, "Do you really want to know?"

"No, but tell me anyway."

Tom had all the Males, 8-10, on the playing field looking for his lost contact lens. By the time the field marshall arrived at Tom's post, the kids had found the lens and Tom, measurable at 6'2" was stretched out full length on his stomach — dramatic in his international orange flourescent ski jacket and lederhosen, carefully reinserting the lens. The scene had the athletes', the spectators' and the director's undivided attention. I can't repeat what the director said to Tom.

The Special Olympics produces all kinds of fun things — you never know what will happen.

One parent confirmed something I had seen but didn't believe. Her child had gotten to the State meets and had the experience of the plane trip, meetings with VIPs, special entertainment, dorm living — all kinds of exciting experiences. When asked by the proud parents whom she had met that impressed her most, the immediate answer was, "Oh, boy! I met Ronald McDonald!"

McDonald's Hamburgers Corporation is especially generous in our state, and obviously the participants appreciate it as do the parents.

I have been involved with Special Olympics myself and know what a day it can be. One meet stands out in my mind — not because of the achievement of the participants (who made out like bandits, getting ribbons all over the place), but by the volunteers. Special Olympic volunteers should get awards. The award I think of now is the "Presence of Mind in the Face of Adversary" Award. I would give it to a young man of 20 who had to subdue a *very* frustrated participant who had chosen to have a tantrum of epic proportions in front of everyone. In the course of the tantrum, the child cut his arm on the watch of the volunteer and the child bled profusely all over the volunteer's white sailing pants. At the sight of his own blood, the kid became subdued and settled down — happy with a small bandage and a bottle of pop. The volunteer, who had the job of awarding ribbons, couldn't find a change of clothes. He had to go on with his job, pants covered with blood.

That was all right with him as he didn't mind our rather tasteless jokes. What got to him was when one of the handicapped ribbon winners very seriously sympathized with him by telling him she was sorry he had cramps on Olympics Day.

He gravely accepted her sympathy, awarded the ribbon, and defied us to laugh.

We didn't — until later.

I have ambivilent feelings about combining "normal"

children and handicapped children in public performances. A little hard to describe but I'll try.

We were recently in a Special Olympics parade and each school and facility was interspersed with local marching bands and various drill teams. It made a very colorful spectacle except for a tiny, niggly, nit-picking thought in my mind. During the Introductions, prayers and stuff, I looked on either side of our particular group and saw to the left a drill team whose specialty included a *high* degree of extraordinary coordination and on the right of us was a crack, precision drill team with straight backs and Prussian stances. Then I looked at our "athletes."

I was holding the hand of one who had the posture of a corkscrew, proudly trying to stand erect enough to show off his Special Olympic T shirt. Ahead of me was another "athlete" who had enough body braces on to qualify as a metal sculpture — and a wave of emotion swept through me that I yelled (mentally), "Unfair competition!"

After years of suppressing these vagrant and unannounced emotions, I was able to swallow hard and say the hell with it. We all went on to have a fun day when our "unfair competition" marched smartly off to wherever drill teams go after performing.

I was swapping notes with another volunteer who had gone with the Special Olympics in another county the same day.

He told me to count my blessings! *Their* parade was led by a personage called "Crazy Joe" or something. This well-meaning chap did this as a "civic service." All staff members, directors and committee members spent the whole day reassuring the TV cameras, the sympathetic public and everyone else that, "*REALLY*, this guy is *NORMAL* — our participants don't and aren't allowed to act like that!

At one point when a group of athletes and volunteers were quietly resting between events, "Crazy Joe" sneaked up behind them and went into a routine that would have had him slapped into a straightjacket and given a shot of Thorazine if he had been "handicapped."

By the way, the participants were a little embarrassed (if not downright frightened) by his "act."

I suspect next year a collection will be taken up for him, as a special treat, to send him to the Azores during Special Olympics week.

Baseball

As I am not known for my shyness, I decided it would be a good idea to invite a Cy Young award-winning pitcher to visit us, give us a pitching demonstration and autograph baseballs. He readily agreed to come and made a major effort to get all the details and description of the program. I immediately rushed down to the nearest book store and took a crash course on baseball, especially about pitchers. When I announced to the program who our guest was to be, they went wild with excitement.

The big day arrived and everyone was there. Also there were 40 very hard balls awaiting signatures. Parents and siblings were out in force, properly subdued because their handicapped brothers and sisters were going to meet the Big Man, touch him, and talk to him. The staff and volunteers had their best duds on and in most cases had even put on shoes.

The magic hour arrived and I wandered out to the parking lot just as he drove up in his copper-colored Mercedes. He got out, dressed like a peacock. We greeted each other and I told him about the fever pitch atmosphere and he said he understood, so was somewhat surprised to walk into an empty auditorium. He had to explain to *me* where everybody was. I had neglected to mention to everybody that this pitcher not only had the sweetest nature in the world but was also a damned handsome male. The whole group were in the johns combing hair (even the guys), covering up acne, checking lipstick, tidying up the kids, using deodorant — prime primping. He and I wandered about the grounds a bit and eventually the gang grooming was accomplished and there they all were. They were as silent as statues, awed with hero worship. The ice was broken when one little boy hollered, "Oh, Johnny Bench! My favorite *catcher*!"

It was then discovered that we had failed to get a catcher's mitt for the pitching demonstration. Someone ran pell mell to the neighboring high school and "borrowed" one. Our guest had all the ladies atwitter and when he asked one to hold his jacket, she went into a trance (her son turned green with envy) and stood clutching it to her bosom. He also let another woman get by with her gushing, "Oh, I'm an *avid* sports fan, and think *all* Heisman Trophy winners are *outstanding* persons!"

Since we were strictly bush, our "catcher" was a guy who had been in Little League or something, and had a long history of adoration for our pitcher. As I had done my homework, I was aware of the lethal potential of a professionally pitched hard ball, so I got everyone secured in safety zones and we were ready for our demonstration.

Here comes the wind up — there's the pitch! His arm barely moved, but I became aware of something passing me like a bullet at the speed of light and hearing an "oof" from the catcher. It was then I opened my considerable mouth and hollered, "He doesn't have protective clothing on!" The catcher assured all of us that he was in great shape and that the pitcher should pour it on him. (Men!) So I told the pitcher it was all right with me if the catcher wanted to be neutered, and besides he was only a volunteer.

The next pitch was a real dilly low one, being caught at about the right thigh toward the inside, so to speak.

The third pitch was the one that got the Cy Young award. It hit the turf going a million miles an hour, bounced up to be caught between the legs and shock set in. The understanding pitcher broke the spell by quietly saying, "And *that* was ball three."

By this time, yours truly stepped in and announced autograph time. I mean, my reputation was bad enough with my agency, and I didn't need "mutilation" on my accident reports. Autograph time was beautiful. One of the sweetest pictures in my mind's eye was seeing this gentle, perfectly formed human being surrounded by children who had less than perfect coordination and treating each as if he were the child of the president. At one point, when in an absent, fatherly gesture he patted the leg of a kid in a wheelchair, he thereby sent one little boy to hero heaven.

We all fell in love eternally with Mike McCormick.

Chapter Nine

Religion and Some *Do*'s and *Don't*s

A meeting was held quite far from earth
It's time again for another birth.
Said the angels to the Lord above,
This special child will need much love,
His progress may seem very slow,
Accomplishments he may not show.
And he'll require extra care
From the folks he meets way down there.
He may not run or laugh or play,
His thoughts may seem quite far away,
In many ways he won't adapt,
And he'll be known as handicapped.
So let's be careful where he's sent
We want his life to be content.
Please, Lord, find the parents who
Will do a special job for you.
They will not realize right away
The leading role they're asked to play.
Comes stronger faith and richer love.
And soon they'll know the privilege given
In caring for this gift from heaven.
Their precious charge, so meek and mild,
Is heaven's very special child.
     (Author Unknown)

MERRY CHRISTMAS

The foregoing was used in a Christmas project of an agency. This is the type of thing I find difficult — *impossible* — to digest.

It is obvious to me that the author of the poem has never *worked* with the handicapped. "So meek and mild" is a dead giveaway. And when it comes to parents, just another theory expert. I won't belabor the above because this *is* really a serene, unbiased, didactic, subjective-negative harangue and I don't want to spoil the mood. However, I personally have offered open dialogue with what Supreme Being is responsible for the administration of this vale of tears we call life.

Religion and handicaps aren't too often entirely separated. The parent can always say that you as a parent are earning your way to heaven or elsewhere by suffering in this life. Or take the opposite tack and say that really Anyone who designed handicaps has to be somewhat maladjusted — not to mention sadistic.

Why is one twin brilliant and the other a mongoloid? Why do two highly intellectual persons have a child with an untestable IQ? Why is the accomplished athlete's son cerebral palsied? Why has the artist a child with useless limbs?

Since it is not a generally acceptable practice to talk back to the sermon, many have given up religious ceremonies when they are unable to shout, "Oh, no, it does *not* strengthen my belief in an Omnipotent Being by His great wisdom in imposing a heavy burden upon my family."

I've always wanted to learn sign language. "Why?" asks the logical reader. Well, as a kid, I used to sit through the services with a group of deaf persons. They had a chap who would stand next to the pulpit and interpret the sermon. They invariably enjoyed the pearls of wisdom much more than the rest of us who could hear the sermon.

Religion and handicapped persons can have some warm moments together. One Sunday school teacher will never forget the day he chose to teach the Holy Trinity. It was the Sunday after Halloween and things were going smoothly. Everyone understood and related to the Father. The Son was appropriately admired and comprehended. Things fell apart, however, at the Holy Ghost.

The Director of a residential facility was asked why an obscure, little-known denomination had 95% of the residents attending services, while the other more powerful denominations had only one or two residents attending. The explanation was that this obscure, little-known denomination had a swinging program and the residents passed the word around. There seemed to be some fickleness, though, as the denomination preferences varied from year to year depending on the clergy, the program, and the quality of the cookies.

Religion can be a great comfort to those who have a firm conviction in it. The author frankly envies the family who can find the necessary spiritual resources in religion and urges everyone who can benefit to take optimum advantage of this gift.

But to return to poetry and at the same time a new subject — if we must have poetry, let's have something that won't bring on immediate retroperistalsis. Let's have some

Edwin Markham.

> He drew a circle that shut me out —
> Heretic, rebel, a thing to flout.
> But Love and I had the wit to win.
> We drew a circle that took him in!

The beloved, long-awaited child has a problem — or gets a problem. Show me someone without any problems and I'll show you St. Michael the Archangel.

The main point to keep in mind is that the handicapped is a person — with all the rights and problems that being a person implies. This is not to say that being a handicapped child or adult is instant candidacy for canonization. Not by a long shot. The percentage of ill-natured, spoiled, demanding, autocratic, and rude handicapped persons is the same as in any other segment of society.

But artificial and unrealistic goals are unfair to anyone.

Mrs. Hefflefinger secretly hates Mr. Hefflefinger because in spite of the fact that she is an outstanding gourmet cook, she is chided by him because she counts on her fingers. Mr. Smith, who is world famous for his work on "Deviant Behavior in Grant Researchers," is highly defensive because he flunked high school algebra and doesn't know a logarhythm from a locomotive.

Haven't you all seen perfectly "normal" children trying their damndest to get maimed by challenging cars on their bicycles? Why should good minds be blown with drugs? Why should 480-hp cars be driven flat out by the cream of our youth? Why would a partygoer, full of "Old Sweatsock" drive home at 2:30 a.m.?

They must all have an unconscious urge to be handicapped.

Think of yourselves. Do you cover your mouth with your hand because you've got a dog-bite scar? Do you color your hair because the real color isn't too "in"? False eyelashes, wigs, padded bras, girdles, cosmetics, custom suits, false or capped teeth, deodorants, vitamins, health foods, strange and esoteric diets — all can be considered as prostheses.

Are we hiding handicaps? Who is to say?

The handicapped child/adult is no different. We are talking about a matter of degree.

I read a list of *Do*s and *Don't*s circulated to an agency staff by the executive director, that I immediately filed under "Clear Thinking." It says succinctly what I have been shambling around *trying* to say.

1. DO — Strong normalization — the idea that the children and adults are more similar to the normal than they are different. All infants should go through *normal* steps in child development.
    a. That community should learn to understand and better accept the handicapped individual.
    b. That the handicapped should strive to accomplish as much as possible what is considered the normal way of doing things.

   DON'T — Give visitors any information, anecdotes, etc., that will make them *pity* the parent or the handicapped individual.

Stress what the handicapped *CAN DO!*

2. **DO** — Mention that the parents' role is especially difficult, more time consuming, more responsibility, etc., but the parents should learn that they can expect the child to learn.
   DON'T — Mention names of either parents or participants.

3. **DO** — Mention that we are interested in programming purposeful activities here at the Center ... individualized as much as practical to help each one better reach potential.
   DON'T — Mention that activities *diminuize* or make the participant childlike or refer to teenagers and adults as "children." We are interested in task performance, not nice "holding" activities.

4. **DO** — Mention that the Center's operation is contingent upon private contributions in time, money, and in kind contribution.
   DON'T — "Poor mouth" ... but indicate that funds are often more difficult to get for operations than for buildings and equipment. Support is encouraged.

5. **DO** — Mention that volunteers and community support are indispensable to the Center.

DON'T — Mention that staff and volunteers are cute, wonderful missionaries or saviours, nor reasons that staff chose to work with retarded. (A "dedicated interest" is perhaps a better phrase.)

(The author fell head over heels in love with number 5.)

6. DO — Mention that CONFIDENTIALITY of participant information is important at the Center.
   DON'T — Link anecdotes or diagnosis with an identifiable child.

7. DO — Talk about specific *activities*, i.e., what the program does and program statistics.
   DON'T — Make "blanket statements" — or how a situation affects the family at home, *nor* make judgmental statements.

8. DO — Schedule *small* groups when possible.
   DON'T — Schedule large groups; they are very distracting. It also creates a feeling of, "Oh, look what the poor handicapped persons can do" (feeling of being on display).

9. DO — Please allow time for questions from visitors directly to the program directors.
   DON'T — Discuss any information with visitors regarding any individual's diagnosis.

Now, reader, isn't that LUCID? The guy responsible for the above should get a raise for this document alone.

I have yet to meet a handicapped person who is personally capable of saying, "Yes, I chose to be handicapped because it strengthens my character."

These persons are to be given *impartial* love or affection and to HELL with any emotional overlay. Pity is the *lowest* form of regard — plus it is non-productive. Self-pity is even more gross. This person isn't benefiting by wallowing in a morass of emotion.

Pull up that head, square those shoulders, suck in the tum — in general pull yourself together and do the best you can when in the presence of a "handicap."

Then you can exchange a glance of complete understanding with your mirror.

FROM THE DIRECTOR'S DESK

Over the past three or four years, there has been considerable discussion surrounding the general usage of the word "retarded." Depending upon who you are talking to, the word "retarded" is considered as educationally appropriate, socially insulting, racially discriminating, a limiting stereotype, or an unjust and unfair generalization.

Whatever the point of view, the word "retarded" is certainly guilty of being greatly over used. It has become a household word and generally has been used in an indiscriminate way to insult someone. Many parents of retarded as well as workers in the field would like to see the disappearance of the word "retarded." However, it is probably more realistic to expect that the word will probably always be around, to some degree.

What should be the approach? Why not low key our conversational usage of labels . . . whether it be "M.R.," "palsied," or "disturbed." The labels, at best, are only convenience labels which often limit both the individual as well as expectations. When describing the handicapped person, why not choose a positive characteristic and comment on that? Everyone will probably feel better because of your sensitivity and awareness.

Chapter Ten

Meetings

We denizens in the handicapped world have to go to a lot of meetings for a variety of complicated reasons that I won't go into. Sometimes I think meetings were designed by coffee producers, manufacturers of hemorrhoid preparations, and other self-interests — held at the scene of the crime and under unattractive lighting.

A professional meeting-goer learns several things. First, the chairs are designed by orthopedic surgeons who do it for a lifetime of guaranteed practice and donated by the local mortuary to remind you that no one is immortal.

Let's look at some of these meetings.

Robert's Rules can be used by the chairperson to subdue any action — but it is a two-edged sword. When told that you are out of order, you can capitalize on this by slamming something down and shouting, "You're damned right I'm out of order! I'm so mad I'm barely rational!"

The Chair may then ask you to leave. The next move takes the nerve of a riverboat gambler, but get ready to leave — huffily and as emotionally as possible. A cape is a great garment of this role. With a hateful, MacArthurish, "I shall return" look at the Chair, start out the door.

The Chair is then put into the position of having to think fast. "Is that rotten person going after the police, going to write the governor with my name prominently mentioned, or — oh my God, the television station!"

There is a very good chance that the Chair will relent, albeit ungraciously, by saying, "If you think you can control yourself, we will touch on your point later in the agenda." At this point you hesitate, hand on door handle, flaring your nostrils and mutter, "I'll be barely under control," and then sit down on the chair nearest the door.

What the Chair often doesn't realize is that when you do get home, you *are* going to call the police, *write* the governor naming names, and *will* get the TV station interested.

This brings us to cameras. Never, never take the presence of a camera lightly. Never. Many people are heard throughout the land saying, "But I didn't take the camera seriously." A sure-fire way to find yourself on the 11 o'clock news, either swinging your notes at a nice little old lady (who is a witch looking like everyone's grandmother), or you can be seen on everyone's TV screen in living color adjusting your bra strap with great attention to detail. I know. I was on national TV seen belting my little kid who looks like an angel.

But to meetings. One learns to be selective. One parent meeting is centered around returning residents back to their facility. Another is centered around the hours their children are being provided a service. The Second Coming could be scheduled and it wouldn't make any difference.

This may be a digression, but I think that this chapter is a good place to say a word (often the temptation is to use a dirty word) about newsletters. Most of us get several, if not what seems like millions of newsletters. Professionals and agencies are placed on everyone's list for the pearls of wisdom that are generated by all groups that can find a typist and a mimeograph machine. Often the typing, the paper, and the subject lead one to believe that it was put together by a university research project teaching chimpanzees useful job skills.

My objection is the turgid prose in newsletters. They can put you to sleep. The reason for the tendency to drop off is the fact that most newsletters say the same thing and appear to be written in code. For example, I received the following bit of information about an activity in which my child was engaged. "This week we have initiated an independent large motor skill exercise stressing concepts of balance and awareness/position in space. Relative movement relationships are critical in establishing rhythms necessary to maintain exercise fluidity. Successful mastering of the movements will enhance self-image as well as increased socialization." I summoned the necessary interest to call and ask what the hell was my kid doing in English and then found out she was learning to roller skate.

In case there are cynics out there I can recommend several books that speak in that same language.

But anyway, let's return to the meetings that generate such literature. Veteran meeting-goers develop a high threshold of pain and a good ear for lies and time wastes.

This brings us to a spectator sport most parents are too timid to play. It is called, "Attending Boards of Directors Meetings as an Interested Observer." A skilled player of this game can up the drug abuse on any board. Most board meetings are open to anyone, but most boards don't go shouting this fact from rooftops — and with good reason.

One loathsome "interested observer" developed a technique that got her welcomed at Board meetings. She would arrive with this big bag, settle herself within eyesight of the most nervous board members (they tend to cling together), and pull out a peculiar-looking craft project. Since no one ever acknowledged her presence they could hardly ask what in all that is good and holy was she building or doing. Meeting after meeting, this project grew in some manner, but never became obvious as to what it *was*. It was never finished and she enjoyed many hours watching the board members twitch.

If you ever get on a Board of Directors, there are some things you should always do. First, get a guest sign-up sheet with two columns — one for *names* and one for *areas of concern*. Pass it around immediately and read it during the "minutes of the last meeting." This simple sheet can clue you about who is watching and maybe why. Having the local syndicated rabble rouser in the audience and not knowing it is dumb if not fatal. Also, do not leave any papers around in neat stacks that you don't really want the parents to see just yet. I got handed a financial breakdown one night because I looked bright enough to be on the board.

The author consistently urges parents to attend boards of directors' meetings. If the Board (who has met regularly for years at precisely the same time and place) starts to show erratic behavior patterns such as meeting irregularly in the timed vault of the local bank (whose president is Finance Chairman), or they cancel meetings because of frequent epidemics, or they declare no meeting because of a lack of a quorum when you walk in the door (even though you personally can count all 48 members) — the board has something on its conscience.

Handicapped agendas often can cause mild hysteria. An outstanding one that grabbed my short attention span was the announcement that arrived in the mail. It was from the Society for the Severely Physically Handicapped, or some such well-meaning group. The notice was to announce a special guest speaker whose topic was, "The Severely Physically Crippled Has Every Right to a Full and Meaningful Sexual Life." It sounded fascinating and I'm sorry my around-the-world tour of native huts conflicted.

One meeting everyone should attend is the one billed as, "Nominations and Elections will be Held." Otherwise, you may find yourself Home Room Mother-Volunteer Custodian for a year. Nine out of ten meetings will put you in a catatonic state (which is just south of North Boring). The *tenth* meeting you will accidentally hear some mumbling that the school/program will close forever and there are no funds until the next century.

The most fun meetings for sheer tension are the dissident parents' meetings. Here the panel consists of *them* and can often be seen mainlining their muscle relaxants while someone adjusts the PA system which everyone knows emits high-pitched shrieks at known intervals. One woman always brought her knitting and became known by *them* as Madame DuFarge — and with some justification, as heads often rolled when she got upset.

I am rarely physically still (vocally, never). Actually, I am only "still" when I'm blindly angry. This trait has given me the reputation of having St. Vitus as my patron saint. All my twitching, fidgeting, flip flopping, head scratching and foot shaking has caused legions of teachers to apply for their sabbaticals. After one meeting, the woman with me said that she knew only one other person who was twitchier than I. He was a young man who was quite attractive. They had to go together to a lot of meetings and he would sit and shake his leg until she couldn't stand it, so she attempted to stop him by putting her hand on his leg. Finally, one night he whispered to her, "What do you suppose the public is thinking when they see us at all these meetings together and you always have your hand on my leg?" She said that was why she resisted the urge to put her hand on my leg.

At another meeting I learned what a research lunch is. You eat while some guys talk. Doesn't sound too traumatic. Well, at my first one the menu consisted of seafood, which I hate. I was reduced to the rolls and the thought of dessert to raise my blood sugar to an acceptable height, while watching wall-sized color slides of genetic problems. I hadn't been paying too much attention to the talk as I was busy trying to get rid of my lunch without a scene. At last the dessert was served (multi-colored sherbet and a cookie). I was just scooping up the first mouthful when I glanced at the wall in time to see an excellent photograph of a baby being delivered — and not by the stork. So much for research lunches. You'll never get me to even *consider* one.

There is a group of about fifty parents who still go into uncontrollable laughter when one merely whispers, "Remember the night we got handed the IUD?" The guest speaker was a lovely, poised and witty woman whose topic was, "Teaching the Retarded the Facts of Life" (always a challenging responsibility).

Everyone, predictably, sat in the back including the teachers. The speaker teased them about this and launched into her talk. The audience knew it was trapped when she said, "No one in this room can say they've never masturbated." Now, who is going to stand up and say, "I haven't," and be considered peculiar. Or worse, say, "Yeah, I do it all the time," and become the Portnoy of the PTA.

To break some of the tension, clever speaker that she was, she then used visual aids and started passing things around for the audience to look at. One startled matron was left unnaturally speechless when the guy in front of her turned around and said, "Look at what I found in my crackerjack box," and handed her an IUD. She immediately cool headedly passed it on to the woman next to her, saying, "Here, you steal it." The woman was a good eight months pregnant and thought she was being ridiculed.

It was a good talk, but the usual vague compliments

that follow such a presentation were hard to think up that night. Something like the banal, "That was very informative," would have branded you as a bit backward, or a "I really enjoyed your slides," might have made you into a latent voyeur. So there you were. A lot of thinkers settled on, "You're a very good speaker."

If you ever get really bored at a meeting, there is one sure-fire way to break it up — or at least a segment of it. Look around for the most pompous, proper, stuffed shirt on the panel. Then in a stage whisper, say to your neighbor, "Do you really believe that 85% of Mrs. Bufforpington's body is covered with love hickeys?" Everyone within earshot will develop strange seizures and find a sudden urge for fresh air.

Any resemblance between these meetings and some you have attended is not coincidental. The same advice applies.

Chapter Eleven

Understanding State Agencies

The author lives in an "enlightened" state — geographically. "Trends" emerge from this state with automobile-assembly-line regularity. I expect massive "trend" recalls any day.

A couple (husband and wife) were registered voters and as such were deemed qualified to check out "licensing" at the state level by their parent organization. So these informed innocents started to the capitol where all state agencies cluster for mutual obfuscation. The couple found the state capitol — it had a golden dome. From then on for them, however, logic went to hell in a handbasket.

This was a simple assignment. Find out what agency was licensed for a certain type of facility and what the provisions were under the new legislation for these licenses.

After an abortive, but hilarious, encounter with the

Motor Vehicle Agency they were referred to Public Housing, which only built but didn't staff facilities. A kindly doorman suggested a Public Health Agency and the receptionist there who was filing (her fingernails) mentioned that they should really be at Voc Rehab. "Of course, why didn't *we* think of Voc Rehab?" During dinner they looked up "Voc Rehab" and got the director's name. Next a.m.: "May we speak to Dr. Donahoe?" (All these agencies are run by doctors and in the enlightened state, all sound similar.).

When the couple's journey was explained, the person in charge said, "Oh, you want Dr. Donahugh of Sanitation and Hygiene." Where was his domain or empire? Only a stone's throw down the hill. Throwing stones in the capital is forbidden.

Dr. Donahugh was in Grenoble at that time, but *actually* it was Dr. Donaven that our couple *really* wanted. They *really* wanted to get drunk and forget the whole thing, but that is beside the point.

Dr. Donaven was in! By accident. He was emerging from the executive washroom when his secretary merrily called to him that his limo was at the Seventh Street entrance. At last our couple found a warm body at the STATE LEVEL. After a whispered conference with his secretary, Dr. D. found he had PARENTS who talked reasonable grammar and had scored by finding him. Psych 1A had taught him to listen at least, and Dr. D. had taken a lot of post grad stuff in Administration, so he busily rallied himself and offered the couple the rotunda's excellent coffee and a chat. (Don't worry about the limo, reader, as the chauffeur of the limo was relaxed and paid hourly plus being immune to double-parking tickets.) Watch caffeine. It is a powerful stimulant. You can get all sweaty, shaky, and in general, pretty well over-revved looking if you accept a cup at each stop along the way. Why do you think it is served to the neurotics on soap operas all the time? All Agency coffee is like the campus beanery's — brewed days before and distilled to brute force, served to the unsuspecting to cause pseudo symptoms of paranoia, piped through the municipal sewer system and served as a "have a cup of coffee." Hemlock is more nourishing.

Yes, back to Dr. D. He *was* informed. My, yes, he could whip out AB 43967B vs. SB 6386 which was gross and *knew* what our couple wished to know.

"However, we are reorganizing and there will be an umbrella or super Agency superceding all licensing agencies and it is in the mill, but parameters or guidelines hadn't been finalized yet but as soon as . . . we'll be in . . . etc."

Why don't we pull the curtain here with our bucolic couple reading tea leaves in the bottom of their cups while the Dr. D's do their thing at many thou a year.

A moment of empathy though. Think how bad these busy directors feel when they are vulgarly exposed to the uninformed, groping amateur who simply cannot even *initially* comprehend the intricacies of the complex mechanism called State Agencies.

Upon learning that State Agencies don't even understand each other, the author (the soul of consideration) will include a couple of suggestions for the reader who wishes to pursue anything at the State level.

First, get a code book and lantern. These can be used

in your search through the thickets of initials, the forests of agencies, and the valleys of depression which always accompany the sincere researcher on the State level. When you have State Agencies figured out, use the attached blank pages to write it all down on.

Then share.

Mail your notes to all the State Agencies, being sure to use simple sentences and short words. I'm sure they will be grateful for this assistance and you will receive their Personalized, Standard Thank-You Form 37X-9A (revised).

Correspondence from State Agencies is cherished by frequent recipients of same. They can be often seen clutching the letters to their bosoms on visiting days. If you want to advance to the federal level, you might want to be fitted for a straitjacket first — just in case.

NOTES

Final Facts

During this writing, the author's mentor posed a series of questions that the author should ask herself. I will try to answer them because they appear quite valid.

Question: Are you bitter?

Answer: With the correct wine I'm considered quite tasty. Oh, you meant *mentally*. No, not really. Being bitter is time consuming and eroding. Without extensive therapy, perhaps you could say I have acquired a bit of a jaundiced outlook with a low credibility factor. But, good heavens! In this day and age, who hasn't? Do you wish to hear what may appear as an unbelievable remark? We are fortunate. Our child is what is known as a "creampuff" in the trade. Our child is physically attractive enough so we may all appear in public without embarrassing ourselves, the child, or the public. Our child is also docile, agreeable, and amenable, so is always accepted instantly in any program. Our child is rather a rarity in the handicapped world.

Question: Have you corrected or changed anything by this book?

Answer: No. It is, however, a neat way to recall a lot of things — the good with the bad.

Question: Who are you writing for? What audience?

Answer: Other closet psychopaths.

Question: What is the last concept you want people to remember?

Answer: I want people to remember that parents of handicapped children are people. Being a parent is a strange job. Consider Mr. Superfurnaceface, corporate whip. He is suddenly thrust in the position of father to Curl Cuteheart. She perpetuates outrages on him that would get her instantaneously fired if she were anything but daddy's angel. Then there is Dora. She got married to some sweet upward-downward mobile guy. She loved him and he thought she looked capable of being reasonably sensible in life.

As individuals we are all right. Then we change roles and become husbands and wives. Big deal. *Then* we become parents! God help the empire. No one of us had any training in the overwhelming responsibility of molding, cherishing, and protecting another life dependent on us.

If you have more than one child, you feel like a juggler — nine oranges in the air and someone hands you the tenth. What do you do? You *do*. It is that simple. I have rarely met a parent who wasn't sincerely doing the best job he knew. Some are unemployed, some separated, some deep in job commitment, some cop out, some develop psychoses, some are right, some are trying and some develop straining coping patterns (such as book writing).

Question: What positive thing is accomplished with this book? What understanding? What attitude?

Answer: I *had* to get this out of my head. Understanding? Well, I just hope those out in the "real" world sort of see that we all share something in common. We are all parents, and as such share much in common.

I heard one mother say sincerely that she was treated as a second-class citizen because she had a handicapped child. That's martyred bullbleep. It is that kind of wooly thinking that gives the rest of us handicapped parents a bad image. She deserves to be drop kicked into oblivion for that. *I'm* not a second-class citizen and I will be damned before I will let anyone else consider me as such.

Question: Will other parents benefit from reading this?

Answer: I think it beats reading your kid's progress reports.

Question: What can the young gain from this book? What can a new parent gain? What has changed in your life as a result of having a handicapped child?

Answer: That's not a question, that's a symposium. It also takes us from the realm of facts into philosophies and I'm not sure I wish to place myself on the lonely pinnacle of commitment.

The young are the most dedicated workers in the field of handicaps that I have ever seen. Their cheer, their lack of stereotype thinking, their boundless enthusiasm, their impartial acceptance of any and all persons have brought tears of pride to my eyes and a huge joy to my heart.

I don't know if a parent who is still in the stunned stage of having a problem will benefit from this book. I *can* hope, however, that they will see all of the beautiful people waiting in the wings on the stage of life poised to help. Believe me, they are there!

I changed the day I was born. All events in a person's life change the individual, so one isolated event cannot be said to change this person. There are so many overlapping forces intermeshing that it would be silly to say that one single thing changed me. One guy told me he will never live inland again. He was a footloose coastal native who decided to try living in Colorado. That got him married, a family, yards of real estate, tons of furniture, the total spectrum of doctors ranging from a pediatrician to a vet, a retirement plan at work and a keen knowledge of deficit spending. All because he went inland once.

The reader cannot help but admire the mercurial ability of the author to slip out of a direct question.

Question: If you had to do it over what would you come back as?

Answer: I would return as the only retarded child of a billionaire and then I would have the world by the tail on a downhill grade.

Question: Are you serious?

Answer: Yes.

Question: Does it appeal to a general reader who would like to know how to better relate to a handicapped child-adult or to better relate?

Answer: I've gone into relatives, but I hope that the general reader will realize that innocent questions or statements can literally tear up a parent. For example, the decision that brings parents to their knees in agony — "residential or out-of-home placement." There are some areas compassionately left unexplored, but please, oh, please, general reader, don't ask in a perky tone of voice, "Aren't you satisfied that you put your child away?" PUT YOUR CHILD AWAY? No parents ever "put their child away." Never.

Also, I don't think a "general reader" exists. In spite of prevailing thoughts, every family I know has a "problem" — be it a handicapped child, a lousy relationship, unemployment — whatever. If everyone at, say, a shopping center were herded into an area and asked, "Do you have a perfect set-up in your family?" there could evolve whole new areas of textbooks. Parents of handicapped children do other things — often quite routinely. I've been recorded as having spent measureable blocks of time not even *thinking* of handicaps. Isn't that callous of me?

Question: What bugs you the most?

Answer: Silly remarks like, "You don't look like the mother of a handicapped child." I've never thought of a suitable reply for that, but I'm working on it. To be fair, I must say I heard a beaut once. We were on a bus after a rally in the capital and were complimenting an especially forceful speaker when someone asked if he had a handicapped child. Upon learning that he did, this voice was heard to say, "Oh, isn't that nice. He has a retarded child of his own!" I made a mental note to up the proof of my anticipated sundowner.

Question: Does it bother you to put your thoughts, experiences, etc., out for general reading?

Answer: Yes and no. It has been an uncomfortable experience admittedly. Mood plays a big part in this. Some days you (your best companion) are as funny as hell. The next day you and yourself are weary of living together mentally and decide to split. Eventually an urge to share something with yourself comes and there you are, chuckling again with the most intimate person around — you and that oddbod you live with: yourself.

Also, don't forget that I had good training for this kind of public disclosure. If some kind of madness propels you in this direction, get a government security clearance. The forms have questions dealing with emergence from the womb until *now* — with attendant references. Do one of those once — while reading the fine print informing you that you flunk out if you forget the name of your elocution teacher in the sixth grade, and your therapist, confessor, or consciousness-raising group, or whatever.

Question: Do you have any last words?

Answer: Always.

It is hard work to be a parent. We all deserve a medal for heroics. As "parents" we exert great power. It is important to remember that, right or wrong, we are doing the best we can on behalf of our children. Do not accept less than that.

This book only endeavors to give a thin smile somewhere. If you see yourselves, don't panic. It is a composite of the greatest group I've ever known — the "I'm *only* a parent" crowd. My fondest regards for your efforts. Also, my regards to your children — after all, without the "perishers" you wouldn't be a parent.

Conclusion

Earlier in the book I mentioned a legendary woman who always wanted a protective mantle to shield parents from further suffering.

I *have* a security blanket. It is made up of 400 wool daises, crocheted together, and it is quite lovely to look at. I made each daisy and did all the crocheting while fighting desperately for a badly needed program. Now I use this blanket to wrap myself up in when my soul is cold. I wrap my children in it when they are frightened or ill. I lend it to friends who are suffering for one reason or another. I've muffled my cries in it; I've hidden behind it, escaped into sleep under it, and I'm not ashamed of any of these facts.

When something comes up that I feel I'm going to be nervous about or afraid of, I simply recall the hardest role I have ever been forced to play.

I had to help the dorm mother catalogue my child's clothes, toys, and treasures prior to leaving our first born. I stood tall and handled each item, mentioning what it was, remembering what prompted us to buy or acquire each. In essence, I was forced to literally relive each day of my child's life in front of a whole dorm full of strangers and the child's grieving father.

I did this ghastly task without shedding a tear, with my shoulders straight, my back erect, my voice unwavering, my head held high, my hands steady. I gave orders, instructions, advice, answered questions, and filled in background.

I then handed my child a picture of the family, said goodbye, turned, and left.

If I can do that, I can do anything.

I spoke of sorrow earlier.

Sorrow is our constant companion on our trip through life. Sorrow gives one a dimension that puts one on a different plane.

Sorrow is cosmic. Sorrow is the blackness of the Universe.

Sorrow can consume.

Sorrow can create.